The Case against Bertolt Brecht

Gerhard Szczesny (pronounced *Ches-nee*) is the author of several studies in philosophy, including *Die Zukunft des Unglaubens* (The Future of Unbelief). From 1947 to 1962 he directed night and special programs for the Bavarian Broadcasting System. He is editor and publisher of *Vorgänge* and *Club Voltaire* and is a member of the P.E.N. club.

SZCZESNY, Gerhard. The Case against Bertolt Brecht; with Arguments Drawn from His Life of Galileo, tr. by Alexander Gode. Ungar, 1969. 126p bibl 68-31457. 4.50

CHOICE   NOV. '69

Language & Literature

Germanic

Szczesny's quest to destroy the myth that Brecht was an enlightened man of progress certainly deserves attention though the evaluations of his harsh and provocative judgment will undoubtedly vary. In his opinion Brecht was above all a Marxist; his idea of the epic theater, his interpretation of history, his anti-individualism and anti-psychologism, his aesthetic concepts — all of this was an expression of faith in Marxist-Leninism. Scrutinizing the three versions of Brecht's *Leben des Galilei* he dwells particularly on the concept of Galileo as a "social criminal," differing radically with accepted interpretations of that term. While Esslin sees Galileo's "crime" in his subordination of science to authorities, Geissler in his recantation for the sake of personal well-being, Szczesny claims that it is Galileo's persistence in pursuing his scientific interests despite his recantation (and therefore a de facto insubordination to authorities) that a true Marxist such as Brecht could not tolerate. The American edition consists only of a translation of Szczesny's essay (rearranged and divided into three chapters) and of a part of Galileo's *Dialogues*. The German version includes three scenes from the first and third version of Brecht's play, the fourth act of Lásskó Németh's play *Galilei* and Reinhold Schneider's essay *Die Monde des Jupiter*. The German text is much more readable than the translation which has a number of unnecessarily awkward constructions and misprints.

183

The Case against Bertolt Brecht

with Arguments Drawn from His *Life of Galileo*

GERHARD SZCZESNY

Translated by
Alexander Gode

Frederick Ungar Publishing Co.
New York

LIBRARY

AUG 1 3 1969

UNIVERSITY OF THE PACIFIC

204326

Translated from the German
Das Leben des Galilei
und der Fall Bertolt Brecht
by arrangement with the original publisher
Verlag Ullstein GMBH, Berlin
Copyright © 1969 by Frederick Ungar Publishing Co., Inc.

Printed in the United States of America
Library of Congress Catalog Card Number: 68-31457
Standard Book Number: 8044-2847-6

Contents

Note on the Textual Affiliations of the Published English Versions of Brecht's *Galileo*

The text of Brecht's *Galileo* evolved through three major phases corresponding, respectively, to (1) the Danish version, (2) the Laughton version, and (3) the published German version.

1. The first version, referred to as "Danish" because it was written by Brecht during his Danish exile in 1938/39, was never published. It was performed in Zurich in 1943.

2. The second version was arranged in Hollywood in 1945/46 by Laughton and Brecht working as a team. It exists only in the form of an English text, performed in 1947 in Hollywood and New York and published by Eric Bentley in 1952 in his anthology *From the Modern Repertoire* (II) and in 1961 in the same editor's *Seven Plays by Bertolt Brecht*. It is also available in a separate edition prepared by Eric Bentley in 1966.

3. The "final" German version is a combination of both the foregoing. It was written in 1953 and first performed (in Cologne) and published in 1955. The 1957 German edition of Brecht's *Galileo* is essentially the same, and so is the text (if not the interpretation) of the 1957 Berlin performance. The third and "final" version was translated into English by Desmond Vesey and published in 1960 by Methuen in London.

For the convenience of the reader, all titles have been given in English. The actual titles of German editions are quoted in the Bibliographical References starting on page 121.

The Case
against
Bertolt
Brecht

I

The Indictment

or **The Dangerous Myth
of the Great Teacher
Bertolt Brecht**

To think of Bertolt Brecht as an "intellectual" (with all the connotations the term has come to convey in our civilization) is a grievous mistake. If Brecht rebelled against the bourgeois world, it was not because it allowed too little but because it allowed too much play for idiosyncratic freedom. He sought the safety of absolute conformism. He was the prototype of the antiliberal thinker. His particular intelligence did not demand independence of judgment in radical logic and upright honesty but reflected a talent for random conceits, that is, for finding a surprising angle in every subject or disposing of it through noncommital "wisdom." Brecht thought in situations and therefore in aphorisms. His philosophy of life consisted of a motley array of recipes for tricking reality. Trickery is an indispensable skill for one intent upon reaching his life's goals without baring their true nature. A man who has made it his concern to hide his identity must at all times keep friend and foe guessing as to his true intentions. His utterances must permit multiple interpretations, his comportment must be hermetic.

If there is among the German writers of the past fifty years one whose life and work require that we apply to them exacting standards, then his name is Bertolt Brecht. We owe it to him that we do not separate the playwright from the student of stagecraft nor these from the Marxist moralist. If we survey, in terms of this global perspective, the part of Brecht's existence which he did allow the world to see, we find that the play the staging of which he undertook with unequaled care was his own life. Brecht did not simply live and work, he undertook to act out a meticulously constructed model case. Throughout his life it was his preoccupation to set up and work out with industrious devotion the scenery, the properties, the situations and the texts for the stage epic, *The Life and the Works of the Great Teacher Bertolt Brecht*. His *Galileo* failed when his concern was no longer to show *The Life of Galileo* but to make of this play a scene in *The Life of Bertolt Brecht*.

Unfortunately, poor Mr. Bertolt Brecht was not at all cut out for the heroic role which he had maneuvered himself into having

2

to play. Sometime in the course of the last few months before his
death he uttered the now famous words preserved for us by his
friend, the Protestant clergyman Karl Kleinschmidt: "Do not
write that you admire me. Write that it was troublesome to have
me around and that I propose to remain troublesome after my
death." The dramatic grandeur of an uncompromising identification with the concept of a radical renewal of the world finally
boiled down to the hope of being remembered as "troublesome."
For a dyed-in-the-wool Marxist, a singularly modest wish. But
this Bertolt Brecht was no dyed-in-the-wool revolutionary. The
struggle of the classes, as it is reflected in his plays, involves in
some cases not even an instruction to the sound-effects man to
come in with backstage thunder. When and where Brecht's plays
are good, they survey the world in critical melancholy, being
demonstrations of life as it is and will be and by no means appeals
to the audience to mount the barricades after leaving the theater.
The man Brecht who stated in Washington that communism and
politics were not his cup of tea but who affirmed in East Berlin—
on that universally remembered Seventeenth of June—his solidarity (however qualified) with the Socialist Unity Party [since
1946 the only political party of the communist German Democratic Republic]—that man was far from being a social hero.
Bravery fared poorly under the tutelage of this master of camouflage. Freedom, to him, was merely another word for bourgeois-
capitalist anarchy, and humanity and humaneness were vaguely
abstract catch-all appellations of a distant and utopian goddess
in whose name every concrete inhuman act committed against a
concrete individual human being could be justified.

It is worth mentioning that Brecht never really understood
or, perhaps, did not wish to understand the true intent of Marx.
Even though there is nowhere in Marx's writings a description of
the state mankind was to attain after the emancipation of the individual from all "self-alienation," [1] the ultimate goal is nonetheless explicitly referred to. It was precisely the removal of all
vestiges of human self-alienation and the total abolition of governmental authority. The demand for world reforms was prompted
by the vision of conditions of life that would permit the concrete

individual human being to live out in full his full individuality.
"Everyone in accordance with his capabilities; to everyone in accordance with his needs." [2]

Man in his state of bondage to external circumstances was a
transitional phenomenon. With Brecht the ultimate goal as seen
by Marx does not come into view. It must not, for through it the
free development of the human person—categorically denied by
Brecht—would appear raised to the status of a supreme ideal.

If there is at all a critical and positive tendency in Brecht's
plays, its aim is the replacement of the societal enforcement of
the individual's social role under capitalism by the societal enforcement of the individual's social role under communism. The
vision of the individual achieving full self-identity does not appear and in fact is explicitly rejected in the theory of the theater
of alienation with its protests against identification and empathy.
Brecht makes the transitional phase of alienation a definitive
stage or ideal. Man is not only now, and deplorably so, "the
sum of the prevailing societal conditions," but he will apparently
always remain thus. Herbert Lüthy [3] stated correctly that Brecht
never evolved "a poetic vision, a concept of endeavor and pursuit,
or even a personal formulation with respect to the content of his
doctrine. Whenever he tries to define what he teaches, he reit-
erates, without change and in tinny monotony, the one shelf-worn
formula which Marx, doubtless aware that it could as well mean
everything as nothing, managed to get along in his theses on Feuer-
bach: 'to change the world.' "

Brecht never was an enlightener. He always was a sentimental
romantic reactionary. He was against the full development of the
human individual "in accordance with his needs." His conversion
from the anarchism of the priesthood of Baal to doctrinaire rigor-
ism was in the last analysis no break. In both, the human person
is denied.

In the 1920s virtually all writers and thinkers with some pretense to progressivism were communists. Only a very few remained
communists. One of these was Bertolt Brecht. This does not signify
that he reached a decision on the basis of a deep conviction
but merely that he had discovered (consciously and/or subcon-
sciously) that the communist doctrine offered him the ideal solu-

tion of the problems of his life. It freed him from the necessity of seeking out personal solutions. It provided a possibility of assuming a humane and humanitarian posture exclusively by virtue of a profession of faith. Finally, it supplied the armamentarium for the kind of dramaturgy he felt impelled to cultivate. With respect to this last point, a fact to be emphasized time and again is that it was not Brecht's profession of faith in communism that became responsible for the development of the epic theater but rather his inability to bring psychology to the stage, and this inability, in turn, prompted and motivated his inalienable devotion to what is at best a popular version of Marxist theory. Brecht was obliged to cling to the end to his role of a Marxist playwright, for his theater of types, which was in fact prepsychological and antipsychological, could claim only by means of its association with a social-revolutionary ideology that it was a metapsychological and avant-garde theater.

This fateful compulsion to ideologize is more clearly apparent in Brecht's *Life of Galileo* than in any of his other works. The *Galileo*, as originally written, was a character drama. In it, Brecht had succeeded in presenting a bona fide individual in conflict not only with the powers of his age but also with himself. Yet Brecht's urge to root out everything subjective and to force the psychological, the complex historical, the unique concatenations of the tragedy of Galileo Galilei into the Procrustean bed of the simplistic patterns of an objectivistic philosophy of history was so overwhelmingly strong that the author himself turned against his work the moment he had finished writing it. This was followed, as we shall see, in two installments by a readjustment of functions involving procedures and yielding results which no longer concern the history of Galileo but that of Bertolt Brecht.

Brecht was a great lyrical and dramatic talent. The full potential of this talent did not come to fruition because Brecht did not succeed in establishing an unprejudiced relationship to himself and to reality. It is tragic, to be sure, that this resulted of necessity in his becoming a second-rate playwright, but still more disastrous in its consequences is the fact that Brecht, past master of trickery, succeeded in outlasting himself in the pose of the Great Teacher. It is because of this that Brecht stands as a justification, as a guide in self-transfiguration to all those who—like him—find no way out of the entanglement of juvenile confusion and then see a solution to all problems in the escape into the Mammoth System. Since we may be certain that several generations to come will continue to seek salvation from the crisis of selfhood and identity in the advocacy of a totalitarian order, it is necessary to destroy the myth of the enlightened man of progress Bertolt Brecht.

Brecht was not a Voltaire or a Diderot; he was not a Lessing or a Büchner. We may apply to him what Sigmund Freud [4] said about Dostoevski: "He missed the chance to become a teacher and liberator of men and sided instead with their jailers. The cultural future of mankind will owe him little."

Brecht sided with the would-be jailers of mankind, pretending to be a teacher and liberator of men.

II
The Evidence

or **Bertolt Brecht's**
Life of Galileo
and the Case against Him

The Three Versions
of Brecht's "Galileo"

Brecht's historical play, *The Life of Galileo,* which—in the stage version now extant—comprises fifteen scenes, was written in the years 1938 and 1939 during the author's Danish exile. In 1945 and 1946, an American version was worked out by Brecht in Hollywood in collaboration with Charles Laughton who had agreed to play the title role. This version was performed in July 1947 at the Coronet Theater in Beverly Hills and in December of the same year at the Maxine Elliott Theater in New York City. There is, finally, a third version in which the Danish and American texts are combined. This final version was begun in 1953, published in 1955, and performed for the first time in Cologne in April of the same year. The Berlin performance of January 15, 1957, the staging of which was directed first by Brecht himself and then by Erich Engel, used a text which differed, it is true, from the definitive published version by nothing more than a number of cuts, but—to quote from the "Remarks on the Closing Scene" by Käthe Rülicke, a disciple of Brecht's who had worked with him as a member of the Berlin company—"it requires the author's stage directions if it is to be complete."

Käthe Rülicke's notes were published in 1957 in the second special Brecht issue of the periodical *Sinn und Form.*[5] Together with other "Miscellanea on Brecht's *Life of Galileo*" they have also been available since 1963 in book form.[5]

Under the title of *Drama and History—Bertolt Brecht's "Life of Galileo" and Other Plays,* Ernst Schumacher published in 1965 a comprehensive monograph utilizing for the first time unpublished documents concerning the origin of Brecht's *Galileo* which are now in the possession of the Bertolt Brecht Archive in Berlin.[5]

Schumacher's study provides, among other things, a thorough and detailed survey of the various drafts and revisions leading to the three complete versions mentioned. There is, for instance, a first (complete) draft preceding the Danish version and differing from it in a number of essential points. Its title is *The Earth Moves*.[6] There are also various textual changes introduced in the 1956 edition in the series of individual plays in comparison with the version published in 1955 in Number 14 of *Versuche*. In our study the text referred to as the original version is that on which the Zurich première of 1943 was based. For the third version we shall be using the text of an edition of 1962 (see Bibliographical Notes), and our information on the production in Berlin has been derived from Käthe Rülicke's notes.

The data compiled by Schumacher indicate that Brecht conceived the plan to write a play on Galileo as early as 1933, that is, on the occasion of the tricentennial of Galileo's condemnation. This plan was part of a more comprehensive project which was to consist of dramatized accounts of great trials in world history. The earliest public reference to what Brecht intended to achieve with his play is to be found in an interview he gave on January 6, 1939, apparently shortly before the completion of the work, to the Copenhagen newspaper, *Berlingske Tidende*. He denied at the time that his play was directed against the political conditions in Germany and Italy and stated: "It was my purpose to depict the heroic struggle of Galileo in support of his modern scientific conviction that the earth moves." He explained that he was not thinking of having the play translated into Danish and performed in Copenhagen, for "it was written for New York." [7]

We know for certain that Brecht consulted members of the research staff of the Danish atomic scientist Nils Bohr regarding the physical and mathematical theories underlying the Ptolemaic cosmology. Such information is indispensable for anyone wishing to understand the revolutionary character of the "Galilean turn of the tide." On February 25, 1939, Brecht entered in his diary the following statement: "The *Life of Galileo* is technically a step backward, just like *Señora Carrar's Rifles*. Altogether too opportunistic. The play would have to be rewritten in its entirety if it is to have something of this 'breeze coming from another coast,' this rosy dawn of science. Everything should be more direct, without the local color of the milieu, without 'atmosphere,' without empathy. And it must all be geared to a planetary scale of demonstration. The structural organization can stay, the characterization of Galileo likewise, but the real work—pleasurable work—could only be done 'at a shop,' in contact with a stage. First the 'Fatzer fragment' and the 'bakeshop fragment' would have to be studied. These two fragments are—technically—the highest standard." [8]

Brecht's doubts about the play he had just finished were thus concerned with aspects of its dramaturgy, not with aspects of its "message" or of the character of Galileo. In this first version, Galileo is characterized as a fighter for progress who introduces a new epoch. The notion promulgated by communist critics [9] that Brecht meant to show in his *Galileo* the situation of the intellectual in the face of the fascist threat is not consistent with the over-all tendency of the play and is clearly denied by the Danish interview already referred to. According to a diary entry of November 23, 1938, Brecht wrote the first version in three weeks: "Finished *Life of Galileo*. It took me three weeks." [10]

In 1940 Brecht fled before the German troops invading Denmark, going first to Finland and shifting his base to the United States in 1941. In July he settled down near Hollywood, in a house in Santa Monica. It was only in 1944, that is, after an interval of six years, that he again began to work on his *Galileo*. The triggering occasion was the interest which the New York stage director and producer Jed Harris had shown in a *Galileo* performance when Brecht visited New York during the winter months of 1943-44.[11]

After his return from New York Brecht tried to interest the English actor Charles Laughton in the role of Galileo. Schumacher wrote in this connection: "It is hard to overlook a certain method in the way the great dramatist prepared the great actor. It was indeed difficult to imagine a more favorable solution for Brecht, whose mastery of English was far from perfect, than to tackle the translation and adaptation together with an actor who, in his turn, knew no German and hence had to express everything by means of gestures." In any event, in the English version emerging from the Brecht-Laughton cooperation, the figure of Galileo appears as consciously cut out for Laughton. Brecht's cooperation with Laughton is the theme of a separate account which Brecht wrote down in 1948 in Switzerland and which was published in 1956. Here Brecht described with what emphasis Laughton managed, in the course of their joint translation and adaptation of the work, to impose his conception of the figure of Galileo. If we may trust Brecht's account, incisive changes of the Danish version were prompted by the actor's wish to make over the Galileo who fought heroically for his discoveries into a vain and cowardly sensualist and opportunist.

In "Building a Part" (the account referred to), Brecht explained: "While Laughton insisted that he must be permitted after the recantation of the thirteenth scene to introduce a great change in the character of Galileo, with criminal propensities coming to the fore, he felt no similar need with respect to the beginning of the ninth scene." [12] Elsewhere in the same account Brecht wrote: "Laughton was eager to show that crime increases the criminal's criminality and insisted, while we were recasting the original play, on having a scene in which Galileo collaborates before the eyes of the audience with the powers that be. This seemed the more indicated since in the course of the scene as a whole Galileo makes the most respectable use of his well-preserved mental powers by analyzing his treason for his former pupil. He dictates to his daughter—to whom in the course of the last weeks he has also been dictating his major work, the *Discourses*—a submissive letter to the Archbishop in which he advises him on how the Bible can be used to keep down hungry workmen. In the process he freely displays his cynicism to his daughter, although he does not fully succeed in hiding the effort which this shameful venture represents to him. Laughton was quite aware of the potentially suicidal temerity involved in his reckless decision to swim against the current by thus abandoning and exposing his figure of Galileo. There is nothing the public is less likely to put up with than this sort of thing." [13]

There are some textual changes within individual scenes. Examples are the rewriting, strictly unfavorable to Galileo, of the ninth scene in which the engagement of his daughter Virginia to Ludovico Marsili breaks up, or the cutting of the tiler intermezzo in the second last scene in which—in keeping with historical truth

—Galileo had appeared as an active conspirator and resourceful fighter against the Inquisition. It is, however, above all the self-accusation inserted in this very scene that makes of the great searcher and scientist a weakling and traitor against the cause of science and of humanity. In the (undated) preface to the American version of *Galileo*, Brecht wrote: "The atomic age made its debut in Hiroshima while we were in the midst of our work. Overnight the biography of the founder of modern physics read differently. The infernal effect of the great bomb placed the conflict of Galileo with the authorities of his age in a new and sharper light." [14]

And in "Building a Part" there is the following passage: "It must be remembered, our performance took place at the time and in the country in which the atom bomb had been produced and utilized for military purposes and in which atomic physics was now kept under a cloak of dense secrecy. . . . Freedom of research, the exchange of discoveries, the international community of science were paralyzed by governmental authorities who were the object of keen distrust. Great physicists precipitously left the service of their bellicose government. One of the most reputed accepted a teaching position which obliged him to waste his working hours on teaching the very first elements of his science. He did so for no reason but that he could not bear having to work under such an authority. It had become a disgrace to make a discovery." [15]

The dropping of the first atom bomb on Hiroshima is regarded by most authors as the true cause for the changes that characterized the American version of Brecht's *Galileo*. A comparison of the dates indicates that this cannot have been so. When those horrifying explosions occurred (in August 1945), the transformation of Galileo into a negative figure, in keeping with Laughton's intentions, had already been decided. The chronologies in the Brecht literature which give the year 1946 for Brecht's collaboration with Laughton are wrong. The two men had begun working together in December 1944. "The atomic age," Brecht wrote in the Preface to the American version, "made its debut in Hiroshima in the middle of our work." According to Käthe

Rülicke,[16] the account, "Building a Part," was written in 1948, that is, after the two American performances. It was only then, that is to say, after the fact, that the Galileo of the second version was linked to the threat of the atom and characterized as a "social traitor."

"Time does not stand still. A new class, the bourgeoisie, had more forcefully appeared on the scene, bringing with it a new industry. It was no longer the achievements of science as such that mattered but the effort to utilize them on a large and all-inclusive scale. This utilization occurred in many ways, for the new class —in order to be able to carry on its business—had to come to power and destroy the dominant ideology which prevented it from doing so . . . for after all, the new class was in a position to exploit its victories in any domain, also in that of astronomy. But once it chose a particular domain as an example and concentrated the struggle on it, it was—in a general way—vulnerable in this area. . . . Galileo became a bearer of harm when he led his science into this struggle and then left the struggle." [17]

In 1955-56, at the time of his stage work for the Berlin performance, Brecht endeavored to emphasize further the characterization of Galileo as a blight unto the people. He did so, without introducing textual changes, by a shift in emphasis and by striking out scenes preserved from the first version but not contained in that worked out with Laughton in America. This applies to the scene of the plague (Scene 5) and to the conclusion (Scene 15) in which the *Discourses* were taken across the border. "The center of gravity of all the changes," wrote Käthe Rülicke, "was in all cases in Scene 13. Apart from organizational changes, such as for instance the shift of Galileo's self-condemnation to the end of the play (where it had the effect of deriding the 'new ethics' of Andrea), the text was also given a considerably more concentrated appearance." [18]

In the minutes of the rehearsal of January 21, 1956, we find the following passage: "Prior to the rehearsal Brecht had a conversation with Busch explaining that the two prior versions—the one showing Galileo as a childish old man, thought with great moments reminiscent of his former intellectual greatness, a man dominated by his daughter whom he had been underrating, and the other showing Galileo in full possession of his mental powers, maliciously making fun of his daughter whose ruin he has caused —presented but two layers of the same figure while Brecht's real purpose tended in a third direction: Galileo was to be shown as a social criminal, as an unmitigated scoundrel. Galileo's crime, as Brecht put it, was made to appear even worse through the fact that, in full possession of his mental powers, he was able to provide a clear analysis of it." [19]

At the same rehearsal he told Regine Lutz, who played the part of Virginia: "Look, Regine, you lead a pitiful life. The thing is this—he is an incorrigible glutton. He eats like a swine, he lives for his body, he is sinful and carnal. You have to excuse everything, yet forbid everything and fight it down. To make matters worse, he is malicious—and you never can tell when he will finally burst out." [20]

Referring to a rehearsal of March 21, 1956, there is this passage: "Brecht once again began the session with an analysis of the figure of Galileo. In previous rehearsals he had been developing the scoundrel; now he drew out the postive aspects of the figure. 'Galileo is presented as a man who is right, as one of the great heroes for the next five hundred years, a man who tramples down everything in his way but who then falls down and turns criminal. That is one of the great difficulties: to show the criminal coming to the fore in the hero. But still: he is a hero, and still, he does become a criminal. That sort of thing you cannot leave to the public. It's you who must bring it out and hope the public will get it.'— 'But remember, too, he is not simply a man who is guilty—it is society which is guilty, for it makes it a crime to be productive. Of course, the Inquisition is more guilty than Galileo, and of course, he must bear some of the brunt. But this must be in it: the man who has fallen, who has done harm to himself by falling, who is vicious and vain, who owns up to nothing, who tries, when the student comes, to sound him out. He is to say something positive, but it just is not in the cards. And he then, with effrontery and provocation in his tone: I am very healthy; I am on my way to regaining my health in mind and soul.' " [21]

"The Life of Galileo"
and the Life of Bertolt Brecht

When Brecht presented the foregoing interpretation of Galileo, some twenty years had gone by since he first began to interest
himself in the subject. In those days, specifically in 1936, André
Gide's settling of accounts with the Soviet paradise had been published, marking the first irruption of skepticism into the enthu-
siastic trust of the leftist-oriented intellectuals in the Russian ex-
periment. The Moscow purges of 1937-38 subjected that trust to a
supreme test. Finally, in 1939, Stalin concluded his pact with
Hitler, thereby throwing off completely the already badly con-
fused antifascist friends of the U.S.S.R., in particular the German
communists. From 1933 on Brecht lived in Denmark. At no time
did he consider the possibility of settling in Russia, although he
was for a number of years, from 1936 to 1939, an editor (together
with Lion Feuchtwanger and Willi Bredel) of the Moscow-pub-
lished literary periodical *Das Wort*. On the contrary, the Copenhagen interview of January 1939 (referred to above) provides evidence for the inference that even then the country he was thinking
of as his real goal and final base of operations for the duration of
the emigration was the United States. The Scandinavian countries
had developed a form of social democracy with pragmatically conservative and in part successful moves by trial and error in the
direction of the classless society; this offered little cause for enthu-
siasm to visionaries of a great communist upheaval. It is an interesting and perhaps significant coincidence that during the early
years of Brecht's emigration, from 1933 to 1936, the Marxist theoretician Karl Korsch was living in Svendborg, in Brecht's immediate vicinity. This Korsch had been excluded from the German
Communist Party as long ago as 1926 because he rejected and
actively opposed Soviet communism, claiming it to be a dangerous
vulgarization of true Marxism.[22]

It is hence quite improbable that the Scandinavian years
corroborated or even confirmed the communist party-line docility
which Brecht had displayed in Berlin. Being an emigré, Brecht
was naturally beyond the reach of all communist party pressures

and assignments, implying a certain detachment in contrast to the
hectic political orientation of his life in Berlin. Indeed, even the
communist interpreters of Brecht's works find it difficult to deny
that his best plays were written between 1936 and 1940 and that
they were his best plays because they were the least dogmatic. It
was during those years that Brecht wrote *Señora Carrar's Rifles,
The Trial of Lucullus, The Good Woman of Setzuan, Mother
Courage and Her Children, Herr Puntila and his Man Matti,* and
The Life of Galileo, the last-named being—from the point of view
of Brecht's aesthetics—his most conventional, his most opportunistic production. Those were the very years during which his
theorizing was at low tide and during which, insofar as he did
theorize, the doctrines of Marxism played only an insignificant
role.

It was only Brecht's American experience that resulted again
in an ideology-oriented trend of both his work and his judgment.
After a phase of antifascist solidarity with the Western Powers
(engaged at the time under the leadership of the United States
in the war against Hitler), Brecht's communist past and, in particular, his personal failure drove him again into opposition to the
bourgeois world. How far the influence which Charles Laughton
had on the revision of *The Life of Galileo* was wanted and invited
by Brecht himself cannot be ascertained on the basis of the available documents. In any event, it is striking to what extent his
description in 1948, in "Building a Part," of his share in the reorientation of the didactic message of the play made it appear a
matter of passive and docile assent, and it would seem—considering Brecht's eagerness and ability to adjust immediately to every
new situation—that we are not entirely wrong if we suspect that
this expression of an attitude of reserved detachment toward the
American version of *The Life of Galileo* reflected Brecht's reluc-
tance to burn his boats.

The première of the American version took place on July 30,
1947, in Hollywood with Charles Laughton in the title role. Compared to the high hopes with which Brecht had looked forward
to this performance, the echo was disappointing. Still, he was not
ready to give up but transferred his expectation of a great success
to the New York opening that was scheduled for December of the

same year. In an interview in September, he revealed his intention
to remain in Hollywood and also expressed his conviction that the
developments in postwar Germany were not of a kind to justify
an optimistic prognosis. Then, toward the end of October, in connection with the public discussion of the influence of communism
in the American film industry, he was summoned to Washington
by the Committee on Un-American Activities and had to submit
to an embarrassing cross-examination regarding his relations to
communism. The minutes of these hearings [23] (of which there is
also a tape recording) show Brecht playing the part of the scoundrel Galileo. He not only denied ever having been a member of a
communist party or ever having had the intention of joining such
a party, he also insisted emphatically that he had never upheld
communist doctrines in his works.[24] His disclaimer was so convincing that the chairman of the committee praised him as a good
example of what a witness should be like.[25]

After this brazen performance, Brecht had no reason to panic.
Yet immediately after his dismissal from the hearings he boarded
a plane for Zurich, not even allowing himself enough time to properly pack his belongings. Early in November he took up residence
in Herrliberg overlooking the Lake of Zurich. Although, while
still in the United States, he had been approached with the invita-
tion to settle in East Berlin, soon after his arrival in Switzerland
he applied to the Allied Control Commission for an entry permit
to Western Germany. It failed to come through, but instead a new
offer arrived from East Berlin. He was promised every financial
support and full freedom in building up an ensemble of his own.
On October 22, 1948, Brecht arrived in East Berlin after a detour
to Prague. In the early summer of 1949 he returned to Zurich for
a stay of several months and then settled for good in East Berlin.
He stayed there up to the time of his death on August 14, 1956,
his last preoccupation being the rehearsals of a performance of
The Life of Galileo.

It has never been determined whether or not Brecht ever
was a member of the German Communist Party. He himself denied it in America. Ruth Fischer (the sister of Hanns Eisler), who
herself had formerly been a prominent member of the Communist
Party, insists that Brecht joined it in 1930. It is certain that he

never became a member of the Socialist Unity Party. He was not even a citizen of the German Democratic Republic but applied as early as 1949—that is, on the occasion of his definitive relocation in East Berlin—for Austrian citizenship. He received his Austrian passport on November 3, 1950. He also managed to secure a special arrangement permitting him to transfer to a Swiss bank account all his royalties and also the 160,000 rubles of the Stalin Prize awarded him in 1954. He was successful in the endeavor to publish his complete works in the West and a commensurate selection in the German Democratic Republic.

It is difficult to overlook the parallels between these events in Brecht's life and certain occurrences in the career of Galileo. The latter left the free Republic of Venice to go to Florence, the ruler of which was answerable to the Church. He did so because he expected to find in Florence more favorable conditions for his work. Brecht found in East Berlin the possibility of setting up an experimental theater in absolute accord with his wants and wishes, affording him the opportunity to pursue his theatrical ideas, without financial worries, in cooperation with a selected group of actors. Galileo denied in Rome his scientific ideal. Brecht denied in Washington his political ideal. Both remained nonetheless faithful adherents of an authoritarian doctrine. Galileo left no doubt as to his faithful devotion to the Catholic doctrine and the Catholic Church. Brecht explicitly saw in Marxism the foundation and the ultimate goal of his artistic work.

Yet, the analogy ceases beyond these few striking points. Galileo recanted in order to save his life. Brecht denied his conviction in order to avoid unpleasantness (and possibly because he enjoyed playing the part of a cunning and crafty trickster). Galileo was convinced that science and the Catholic faith were compatible, assigning to them separate domains of competence. For Brecht, his Marxist faith was the ultimate basis of his literary endeavor, permitting no segregation and no restriction of competence. Galileo had desperately tried to induce the Church to recognize the validity of his scientific discoveries. Brecht knew all along that the communist state cannot and will not admit an independent science or an independent art. If Galileo were no hero, Brecht certainly was even less of one. If Galileo can be accused of having betrayed the freedom of science, Brecht still more betrayed the freedom of art. One cannot but suspect that Brecht himself must have sensed the reality of these parallels, and this raises the question as to why he returned twice to this (to him) highly delicate subject, being unable to relinquish it to the very end of his life.

This is a decisive question. In order to answer it, we need to sort out the possible uses a dramatist could make of the historical subject of Galileo and to ascertain which ones were taken up and made to occupy the center of stage by Brecht and where and to what extent he deviated from historical truth.

How the Fighter for Progress Came to Be a "Social Criminal"

In his preliminary studies for *The Life of Galileo*, Brecht utilized what is still today the most important source on the subject available in the German language. This is the first volume of Emil Wohlwill's *Galileo and His Fight for the Copernican Doctrine* of 1909. It is probable that Brecht also knew the second volume of this work, which was published in 1926, and the book by Leonardo Olschki, *Galileo and His Age*. According to Schumacher [26] Brecht also had on hand the two-volume German translation of the *Discourses* by Arthur von Oettingen. From it he took over verbatim quotations. What all this proves is that Brecht was fully informed of the historical data in the case of Galileo Galilei.

It goes without saying that the poet and dramatist has the right to interpret in his way both historical characters and historical events. But the freedom he enjoys in this respect is not unlimited when his objective is to present a great figure of history in its historical importance and not—as was Shakespeare's objective in his historical plays—to portray individual characters and their fates. Brecht's objective in his *Galileo* was precisely to show a great historical figure in its historical significance. Brecht did not say: the figure I have made up for myself and decided to call Galileo is a scoundrel. On the contrary, he was most emphatically concerned in showing in his play the failure and the crime

of the real Galileo. This implies that he invites a comparison of
the figure created by him with the historical Galileo. His interpretation is either correct or wrong; it either presents historical
truth or is historical shadowboxing. The range of poetic license
still available to him concerned the characterization of secondary
figures, the selection, manipulation, and even invention of individual scenes, and the interpretation of the available documentation on the character of the hero insofar as it is subject to variation
depending on the interpreter's point of view.

The less authentic material there is the greater becomes the
range of poetic license; the more material there is, the more
strictly is the author tied down to a fixed character portrait and
a fixed historical continuity. As Ernst Schumacher put it in his
essay "Form and Empathy," which is specifically concerned with
Brecht's *Galileo*, "It was possible to put a frame around history,
but it was not possible to treat it as a collage, as can be done with
invented stories. The basic attitude, the social habitus, was predetermined by history and could not be 'posed.' It was not possible to freely create a gestic table to represent the social habitus
... for the gestures were predrawn in the tables of history." [27]

This then makes it pertinent to ask what thematic conceits
and what possibilities of interpretation are inherent in the historical Galileo. There is first of all the theme of the obscurantism
of the medieval Church which did not shrink back from the use
of force whenever it saw its power over men threatened. Then
there is the theme of the triumphant march of victory of scientific
knowledge in the world of reality, which no terror and no oppres-
sion was able to stop. A third theme is the definitive break between faith and knowledge seen as a consequence of the blindness
of the Church (with the possible collateral topic of the Catholic
countries lagging behind the Protestant leadership in the dawning
phase of the age of science and technology). As a fourth theme
we see that of the great scientist who feels no call to martyrdom
and prefers to save his life and the possibility of going on with
his work by an attitude of passive assent and submission. Finally,
if the point of view of the interpreter is that of a conservative
Catholic, there is the fifth theme of the world of man emerging

through new knowledge from the sheltered safety of the past, falling away from God, and drifting toward an ultimate doom.

In Brecht, the first of these themes—that of the power of the church—plays surprisingly no role worth mentioning. The second theme—the triumph of science—has only marginal significance, being relegated, as it were, to the dim illumination in the wings. The third theme—that of faith versus knowledge—never comes up for discussion. Nor does the fifth—the theme of the falling from grace through knowledge. It is the fourth theme—that of the unheroic scientist—which is moved to the center of the stage, though in a form that has not only been stylized to achieve a more concentrated dramatic effect but that has also undergone incisive modifications. Brecht's Galileo is not simply nonhero; in the end he becomes a "social criminal" and a "scoundrel." This he becomes because—as Brecht wants to have it—his capitulation before the authority of the Church must be regarded as the "original sin" of modern science.[28]

The changes which the play underwent from the Danish first version to that used in the Berlin performance show that the point is not that Brecht in the course of those six years arrived at a different opinion of the character of Galileo because new historical material had come to his attention or because he had come to see the old material in a new light but simply that Brecht had decided in favor of a different interpretation of Galileo's recantation. The procedure as such is in no way objectionable; it is, indeed, quite consistent insofar as Brecht was at all times emphatic in his insistence that he was not concerned with characters and that to him the only matter of interest was a man's comportment, i.e., his social role. The procedure does become strange and dubious, for value judgments such as "criminal" and "scoundrel" are concerned after all with character traits, that is, they involve verdicts relative to the subjective qualities of an individual, regardless of the objective consequences which those qualities may or may not entail. We must concede that at least the concept of a "social" criminal implies to a certain extent that the criminality in question is not what the term implies in its conventional acceptation in the frame of reference of individualistic morality. But all the other epithets used for Galileo can only suggest that he was in every sense a worthless individual, a coward and weakling, a lecher, and a cynic.

But there is an additional complication. The Galileo we meet in Brecht's play is by no means as depraved as the one whom Brecht tried so very hard to develop from it through his work as an interpreter and as the stage director of his own play in Berlin. Brecht would have had to rewrite the play from start to finish, and in utter disregard of the historical documentation, in order to change the Galileo of the Danish version into the fiendish monster which the aged scientist reveals himself to be in self-condemning terms in the revised thirteenth scene. Since he did not do so, the changes introduced in 1945 into the original version of 1938 merely made of the courageous fighter for a new era a two-faced character with, to be sure, a striking emphasis on the shady aspect of it but implying also that the possibilities utilized by Brecht to impose a negative interpretation on the figure, which had been strikingly positive in its original conception, were extended to the ultimate limits of credibility and perhaps beyond. In order to show a social criminal and scoundrel with convincing effect, Brecht would have had to proceed much more ruthlessly in his textual revision. As things stand, the figure that had come to life in 1938 proved stronger than all subsequent attempts at changing it through interpretation and staging techniques.

A critical study of the available source material proves that the Galileo of the original Danish version came closest to the historical Galileo.[29] Historically Galileo was neither a criminal and scoundrel nor the full-blooded swashbuckling cynic that the full-blooded swashbuckling Charles Laughton wanted to present him as on the stage. The full picture of the character of the historical Galileo cannot dispense with precisely the scenes that were changed or omitted in the second version. In the Danish version of the eighth scene (the ninth by the later count), Virginia herself breaks off her engagement to Ludovico whose narrow-minded egotism has become apparent to her through a heated exchange of words between him and her father. She does not faint, nor does she reproach her father either directly or even indirectly. The scene is laid out in such a way that the dissolution of the engage-

ment does not appear as the fault of Galileo but provides the
occasion for the character of Ludovico to be revealed in all its
shabbiness in confrontation with Galileo's understandable zeal
to resume his studies. And again, in the concluding scene of the
original version, we neither meet a Virginia who had become "a
sour old maid" nor a Galileo who, as her father, derides and de-
ceives her. What he dictates to her is not a sanctimoniously servile
letter to the archbishop but a passage from the *Discourses* and
the entire scene is pervaded with the feeling that father and
daughter are linked by strong bonds of affection, even though
Virginia is understandably worried lest the visit of his former
student might excite him too much and might, indeed, prove
dangerous to him. In Berlin, on January 20, 1956, all this looked
as follows: "Brecht is trying out a version radically different from
the first. He shows Galileo as a man in complete possession of his
powers, who does give in to Virginia to the extent that he dictates
the letter but who treats her with irony and scorn. 'I rely entirely
on your better judgment,' he says with unconcealed sarcasm. In
human terms this makes him more negative; he has not only
wrecked Virginia's life, he goes on to amuse himself at her expense; but in intellectual terms he is thus made to keep the upper
hand." [30]

In the same scene (that is, Scene 13 of the earlier and Scene
14 of the later version), the two passages that were suppressed in
1945—the monk's allusion to Galileo's continually smuggling manuscripts out of his confinement and the conversation with the tiler
whose services Galileo utilizes to have his manuscripts get out of
the house behind the back of the guards—are fully in agreement
with the historical truth. A very few weeks after his condemnation, Galileo had indeed begun to seek contacts that would enable
him to have the dialogues, for the sake of which he had been
condemned, taken out of Italy with a view to getting them printed
abroad. These cleverly worked-out and promptly implemented
schemes to deceive the all-powerful Inquisition were not the do-
ings of a coward. Galileo knew that he was entirely in the hands
of the Inquisition. What was in store for him in the event his
efforts were discovered was possibly not death at the stake but
certainly torture and imprisonment. Two months before Laugh-

ton was to undertake to prove to the New York public what a
conclusive demonstration of his utter lack of character and in-
tegrity Galileo had provided by not hastening to invite torture
and imprisonment for the sake of mankind and progress, Brecht
did hasten to try as best he could to convince the American investigators that he was a harmless citizen and had nothing to do
with communism in particular or with politics in general.

Surely, the fact that the historical Galileo was no weakling,
no lecher, and no cynic, as the American version, and still more
the Berlin staging, were making him out to have been, this fact
—though making the play questionable as a character study—
would not in itself be sufficient reason to reject it as a credible
interpretation of the case of Galileo, that is, of the historical significance of his discoveries and of his "failure." The fatal ab-
surdity of Brecht's Galileo, that is, of what Brecht wants us to see
in Galileo, is the very specific and, to put it mildly, the extremely
peculiar accusation that the great scientist was a "social" criminal.
What Brecht regarded as Galileo's social crime has been described
by Käthe Rülicke at the beginning of her "Remarks on the Closing
Scene." He (that is, Galileo), she explained, "built up a new
physics, but he destroyed the productive utility of that physics.
He came to be the technical creator of new productive forces, but
he also came to be their social traitor. He provided the revolutionary theory, but he was unable to cope with its practical implications. Even though he supplies an analysis of his case and thus
a warning to coming generations, his work cannot make up for
the damage that his treason has inflicted on society. That he hands
over the *Discourses*, although his motive is vanity, does represent
a service to society which, in the person of Andrea Sarti, presents
its rightful claim to take over the book. Yet, Galileo speaks the
truth when he says: 'A man who has done what I have done cannot
be tolerated in the ranks of science.' " [31]

Käthe Rülicke's report, first published in the periodical *Sinn
und Form* in 1957, is included in the collection of documents on
Brecht's *Galileo* of 1963 in a form which, as the "Notes" to the
volume (p. 211) put it, was "slightly abridged," though in fact
the "abridgment" amounted to changes in textual substance. According to the 1963 version, Galileo "impeded" and did not "de-

stroy" the productive usefulness of his physics, and the "technical creator of new productive forces" became the "creator of new productive forces." Since the notes of Frau Rülicke have the character of a "record of the proceedings" and since her comments were made under the immediate impression of the rehearsals in 1956, it seems sound to assume that her interpretation as presented in 1957 came closer to Brecht's real intentions than the text of 1963. In any event, at this later date, Frau Rülicke—or the editor in her stead—felt the need to soften the accusation that Galileo "destroyed" the usefulness of his physics to the reproach that he "impeded" it. The reason for this change is doubtless the very same that makes it difficult for the unprejudiced and unindoctrinated reader of Brecht's verdicts on Galileo to understand what all the fuss is about, and, indeed, to understand the meaning of the reproach leveled at Galileo.

After all, what Galileo "destroyed" or, if we prefer, "impeded," was—if anything at all—an underlying concept of theoretical science but certainly not "the productive usefulness of his physics." His recantation and "betrayal" did not concern the technical exploitation of his discoveries but their theoretical and rational core. The fact that the Copernican cosmology had been rejected prevented no one in the Catholic world, including Italy, from blithely making use of the celestial charts worked out on the basis of the Copernican system, and in precisely the same way no substantial delay in the spread of the technical advances occasioned by the theoretical insights and the practical investigations of Galileo can be claimed to have occurred in consequence of his difficulties with the Church and his subsequent recantation before the Inquisition. It is true, the center of gravity of research in science and technology shifted in temporal coincidence with the trial of Galileo to the northern Protestant countries, but at no time did the Church interfere in the use of techniques or of instruments related to Galileo's discoveries and investigations. His writings, it is true, were kept on the Index up to the year 1832, but the "productive utility" of their concepts was allowed free dissemination and full exploitation during Galileo's own lifetime throughout the Catholic world as well, with no exception to be made even in regard to Italy.

What then is the "social treason" committed by Galileo? What is the "practice he could not cope with?" Was it his duty to anticipate the French Revolution or to draft a communist manifesto? When we bear in mind what Western society was like around 1600, we cannot but regard such a suggestion as ludicrous and, indeed, perverse. It was the time when the great colonial empires were being established. Early capitalism was still in its infancy, and the class system of the feudal order was still going strong. There were peasant uprisings, and the urban masses did manifest a smouldering kind of discontent, but there certainly was in no sense a concretely political frame of reference for the instigation of a revolution of the bourgeoisie, of the peasantry, and least of all of the proletariat of a kind that would have been in keeping with the democratic principles that were potentially inherent in the new cosmology. The street-singer scene of the first version of 1938 is not unhistorical, for during Galileo's lifetime it was indeed not unusual for Italian carnival pageants to represent astronomic themes, and it is wholly conceivable that Galileo's discoveries, too, were dramatized in this fashion. An entirely different matter, however, is the tendency manifest in the later substantially altered and strikingly more radical version of this scene which suggests to the audience the notion that a steadfast Galileo could have become a leader of the masses, that he could have made a people's republic out of the Italy of city states and principalities and papacy, a people's republic with 1633 as the year of its birth. This is devoid of even a semblance of credibility.

But even if we assume for argument's sake that such a revolutionary upheaval was within the realm of possibilities, there still is nothing to justify the demand that a scientific genius such as Galileo should have been—in that century, under those conditions —a political genius as well, or even that he should have been a politically oriented contemporary. The "criminal" role of Galileo emerges from the fact that Brecht placed him in a historical situation that in the Italy of the early seventeenth century simply did not exist, that he demands of him a preoccupation with problems that to conceive of, let alone to pursue, was utterly impossible for the historical Galileo. Ernest Schumacher, whom we have repeatedly quoted, reached the same conclusion after a detailed analysis of the political conditions prevailing at the time in Italy. "In sum, we may say," he wrote, "that Galileo did not commit the social treason which Brecht imputed to him in the revised version of his *Life of Galileo* and, in particular, in his notes to the play." [32]

As one traces the metamorphosis undergone by the *Life of Galileo* from its first version to the staging in Berlin, one is forced to observe that an originally coherent and cogent presentation of historical veracity has become, through a smothering overlay of doctrinaire theses, a paragon of confusion.[33] In the Danish version of the self-indictment (in the thirteenth scene), Galileo defines the task of science as the obligation "to subordinate not fact to opinion but opinion to fact." And he condemns himself by stating: "Science has no use for men who fail to enter the lists in the name of reason." In the American version no trace is left of this implied profession of faith in reason and in facts. Now the point at issue is the responsibility of science in the unmasking of the "machination of princes, landowners, and clergymen" and the "fight of the Roman housewife for milk." And the essence of scientific work is now defined by the statement: "I contend that the sole goal of science consists in easing the hardship of human existence."

What is it then that was betrayed by Galileo? The truth of science? Reason? Mankind at the mercy of a science "piling up information for information's sake?" Or is it that he neglected to become the liberator of Italy? "As a scientist I had a unique possibility. In my time astronomy reached the marketplace. Under these very special conditions, one man's steadfastness could have provoked a major upheaval." Was it, more restrictedly, the "code of ethics" of his profession that he betrayed? "Had I resisted, science might have developed for its adepts something like the Hippocratic oath of the physicians, the pledge to use their knowledge exclusively for the benefit of mankind."

The perspectives of treason are not only multiple, they are mutually contradictory. A science dedicated to facts and reason will someday produce milk powder, but it can hardly be held responsible for the price of milk at a particular time. And if it feels the obligation to march straight ahead toward the goal of the happiness of man, it will of necessity collide with views that regard too inconsiderate a dissemination of "facts" as a source of unhappiness. Precisely this the little monk has in mind in Scene Eight (Nine in the later version) when he warns Galileo against the dangers to mankind that are inherent in "too restraintless a form of research." From this point of view one cannot but regard as wise the measures the Church undertook against Galileo, for it was their objective to preserve the people's peace of mind. In her Galileo novella Gertrud von le Fort gave expression to this point of view when she had the Cardinal say: "Your master is not in need of your intercession. In my heart I pronounced him not guilty long ago. Yet, there are men who—though themselves unimpeachable—represent nonetheless vessels of dangerous seduction. Rest assured, these Medicean stars will be followed by others—stars of fright will rise on the horizon of mankind. [. . .] What I saw in those moments was the man of the future. Just as this unfortunate girl has conjured up her own destruction, so someday mankind will conjure up the destruction of the world. For knowledge will always have to be paid for with death. It was thus in Paradise with Adam and Eve, and thus it will be forevermore." [34]

In the eyes of the little monk Galileo was a "social traitor" long before Brecht expressly called him that. And the question imposes itself whether it is possible that Brecht failed to see this analogy. The question will come up again in a later context.

Consider now this handy handsome formulation: "As things now stand, the most that can be hoped for is a generation of inventive dwarfs who can be hired for anything." The formulation has become part and parcel of the thesaurus of quotations that are a stock-in-trade of the moralizing columnist, but it is certainly not applicable to Galileo and the scientists of his time. It simply is inconceivable that they should ever have worried lest their astronomical and physical discoveries might involve disastrous consequences. They could not but be convinced that what they found in their probings would accrue to the benefit of mankind. After all, what they were after was not the invention of gunpowder or the guillotine. Galileo and his scientific peers in the Europe of his time felt their obligation to facts and reason. This is a point that the Brecht of 1938 was still able to understand. Galileo's peers disseminated Galileo's discoveries as best they could. And their scientific ethics did not suggest to them that they might condemn Galileo, for to them it was both natural and meaningful that he saved his life and ascribed a higher value to the possibility of continuing his studies than to the abstract demand of ideological steadfastness.

The prophesy of the "dwarfs who can be hired for anything," which Brecht in 1945 put into the mouth of Galileo, is historically absurd and exemplified by the most inappropriate object imaginable. For that reason it does not promote but harm the ethical strength of the appeal to the sense of responsibility of the scientist, which in our days is indeed not only justified but an inescapable necessity. If we are honest in our probings of the problem we cannot but recognize that the question of conscience arises for the scientist only when a discovery of his is about to be exploited for the ends of evil. There are certainly few if any discoveries and inventions that have not at one time been pressed into the service of the technology of war and murder. When, for instance, Otto Hahn and his collaborators tried to unravel the complexities of nuclear fission, it was no doubt the scientific problem as such that provided their motivation and possibly the prospect of the discovery of a new immense source of energy for the benefit of mankind. Similarly the American atomic physicists back in the fateful years of 1944 and 1945 were no "inventive dwarfs who could be hired for anything." They were investigators who found themselves—through the complexities of the struggle of the free world with Germany and Japan—confronted with a situation that was intrinsically tragic, and neither the situation itself nor its tragic implications were imposed on the scientists by the American government. In a communist state, to be sure, scientists cannot and need not be "hired." They are civil servants and are not given the slightest chance to invoke in cases of doubt a Hippocratic oath. Those eighteen nuclear physicists in the Federal Republic of Germany who publicly declared in April 1957 that they would not in any way take part "in the production, the testing, or the use of atomic weapons" did so on the basis of a personal decision. If ever a situation arises that puts their steadfastness to the test, it will not be within the powers of the Federal government to prevent them from heeding the commands of their consciences.

The fourteen nuclear physicists of the Federal Republic of Germany who were heard from one month later expressed themselves much more noncommitally, contenting themselves with a general proclamation of their peaceful intentions: "It is our wish that the nuclear processes shall be made to serve the life of mankind and that they shall not be misused for its destruction." Whose wish is otherwise? None of the fourteen will be compelled to recant if the day comes when he is ordered in the Democratic German Republic or the Soviet Union to participate in the production of atomic weapons for indeed such weapons would serve the objectives of world revolution and "the life of mankind."

Still worse, the anachronistically political appeals to conscience which Brecht put into the mouth of his Galileo cannot even be claimed to have the value of a statement of principle favoring peaceful intentions, for Brecht was no dewy-eyed humanitarian ecstatic but a Marxist who placed the greatest emphasis on the need for a pronouncedly brutal and realistic approach to the facts of history. Seen in this light, the moralizing political postulates of *The Life of Galileo* are not merely anachronistic and contradictory, they are vacuous bits of rhetoric of a soapbox demagogue. They postulate for the scientist rules of conduct of which Brecht knew very well that their claim to being taken seriously as ethical maxims was predicated on the ideals of precisely the bourgeois society that Brecht fought so uncompromisingly and without letup. Brecht's ideological redrawing of the figure of Galileo thus involves forgery on two counts. It imputes to a scientist of the early seventeenth century the conflicts of conscience of the atomic physicist of our day and formulates demands whose ethos does not reveal but in fact conceals the true political goals of the author.

Under the circumstances Galileo did in fact the utmost as well for the cause of science and mankind as also for social progress. Had he refused to recant, he would have been incarcerated under conditions excluding the possibility of his writing the *Discourses*. And it is precisely this work of Galileo's that formulated principles of the physics of solid bodies and of motion that were of decisive significance for the future "productive utility" of the Galilean revolution. And even if it could be shown—though the available documents make it a highly dubious attempt—that Galileo's only reason for recanting was that the prospect of being tortured by the Inquisition frightened him, his behavior would still be no "crime" or lessen the positive value of his endeavor, after his capitulation before the Inquisition, to do everything in his power to go on developing and disseminating his new scientific concepts.

If it is at all possible to speak of guilt in this context, then Galileo's guilt is a matter of individual ethics that concerned only him as a human individual. To pronounce Galileo guilty by an exogenously objective dictate is inadmissible not only for the reason that martyrdom can never be a moral demand made by us upon others but also for an additional reason that Brecht managed to suppress entirely. Since Galileo was and wanted to be a good son of the Church and a devoted Catholic, his submission does not merely signify that he did swear to the truth of something he knew to be untrue, it can also be interpreted as reflecting his genuine sense of obedience toward an authority that in this specific case, to be sure, handed down a verdict regarded as false by the condemned but whose wisdom and competence were acknowledged by him as a matter of principle. Galileo considered the Bible to be indeed the font of true faith. He merely rejected the notion that the Bible was a textbook of astronomy.[35] In the concluding act of the Galileo drama of the Hungarian writer László Németh, this personal conflict of Galileo is analyzed, and in Reinhold Schneider's outline for a play on Galileo, the central theme is Galileo's need to come to terms with the Aristotelian theology which he wished to see replaced by a Copernican theology. The Brecht of 1938, too, saw and presented a Galileo with traits of the historical prototype.

And, finally, neither in America—if we may disregard Laughton's personal wishes—nor in Berlin was there an externally imposed necessity for Brecht to change the original version of his *Life of Galileo*. He could very well have played the Danish version not only in Hollywood but also in East Berlin, with the exception (in the latter case) of certain passages that would have been understood as attacks upon the German Democratic Republic and the Socialist Unity Party (as, for example: "Up there the darkness has grown even darker. Beware when you travel through Germany carrying the truth under your cloak."—Scene 13 of the first version), for in East Berlin, too, the portrayal of a great scientist's heroic struggle for progress and against the Church would have been hailed. Thus we cannot but conclude that the motivation for Brecht's ideological redrawing of the figure of Galileo must be looked for in Brecht's personal convictions. And these personal convictions cannot simply have been a matter of his partisan acceptance of the Marxist approach to history (though this acceptance did again become more pronounced and manifest during the latter years of Brecht's stay in America), it must also involve—inseparably intertwined with his political creed—the principles and opinions upheld by Brecht in matters of aesthetics. As early as 1939, it will be remembered, the playwright Brecht applied to his own *Life of Galileo* the remarkable epithet "opportunistic." We shall thus have to concern ourselves briefly with Brecht's theories of the theater.

A Theater for Fruit Pickers
and Motor-Vehicle Construction Engineers

In an interview of July 30, 1926, that appeared in the periodical *Die literarische Welt*, Brecht summarized for the first time his aesthetic principles: "My poems are personal and private. . . . In stage plays, on the other hand, it is not *my* mood that I present but, as it were, the mood of the world. In other words, in my plays I present things viewed objectively, the very opposite of mood in the ordinary and poetic sense of the term . . . I do not allow my feelings to insinuate themselves into the processes of playwriting . . . I appeal to reason. . . . My goal is the epic theater. . . . I merely present events in order to induce the public to think."

In 1932, in the notes to his play *The Mother*, Brecht formulated a "non-Aristotelian dramatic theory." Here the presentation aiming at factually objective documentation, with the goal of showing the world as it is, appeared modified by a political didacticism through the stage in the service of a Marxist ideology. "The

spectator is treated as being confronted with portrayals of specimen types in such a way that he is dealing in full reality with their
prototypes, provoking them to make utterances and to carry out
acts, and that he cannot and must not regard them as strictly and
fully determined phenomena. His function and duty in the presence of his fellow men is to become himself part of the complex
of determining factors. These—that is, the determining factors of
the social milieu, of specific occurrences, etc.—must hence be
treated as variable. A certain substitutability of the events and
circumstances must present the spectator with the possibility
and obligation of effecting assemblies, of experimenting, and of
abstracting." [36]

The "alienation effect" appeared for the first time in Brecht's
writings in 1936 in the article "The Theater as Entertainment
versus the Theater as a Teaching Institution." Here we find the
passage: "In no way was it possible any longer for the spectator
to abandon himself, on the basis of a simple empathetic identification with the dramatis personae—uncritically (and hence in-
consequentially)—to an experience. The presentation subjected
the topics and the events to a process of alienation. This was the
alienation that is a necessary prerequisite to comprehension. In
'what is self-evident,' comprehension is simply dispensed with.
The 'natural' had to be imbued with an element of shock. There
was no other way of having the laws of cause and effect stand out.
What was required was that the acts and actions of the figures on
the stage had to be what they were and simultaneously could have
been otherwise." [37]

And finally in his last major piece of writing, the "Small
Organon for the Theater" of the year 1948, he once again summarized the various viewpoints of his theories of the stage in a
series of autonomous aphorisms:

"20.   What brings science and art together is that both exist
for the purpose of making man's life easier, the one preoccupied
with sustaining, the other with entertaining him. In the age that
will come, art will derive entertainment from the new produc-
tivity which will be able to sustain us so much better that it may,
when unimpeded, be the greatest entertainment of all.

"22.   Our representations of how men live together are

worked out by us for raft builders, fruit pickers, motor-vehicle construction engineers, and social rebels whom we invite to our theaters and urge not to forget their gay interests while we have them with us, for we propose to turn the world over to their brains and hearts in order that they may change it as they see fit.

"43.   The sole purpose of these new alienations was to deprive the socially moldable processes of the hallmark of familiarity which now shields them from any intervention.

"55.   . . . but the supreme decisions in matters of the human race are fought out on earth, not in the air; in 'externals,' not in men's heads. No one can stand above the classes and their struggle, for no one can stand above men. Society has no common spokesman or mouthpiece so long as it is divided in struggling classes. So 'to be nonpartisan' can signify to art only to belong 'to the ruling party.'

"65.   It is the 'fable' that is all-important; the fable is the core of the theatrical venture. For it is from what occurs between men that men derive all that can be discussed, that can be criticized, that can be changed . . ." [38]

The epic theater, the non-Aristotelian dramaturgy, the alienation (or exotification) effect—all these concepts in Brecht's aesthetics are ideologically oriented. They do not simply represent theories concerned with questions of acting, staging, performing; they are pillars and keystones of a universal doctrinal system of societies and Society—that of communism. Specifically, the system is what the initiates like to call "vulgate" (or even "vulgar") Marxism. Brecht managed to make do with three theses: 1. History has so far been a history of class struggles.   2. What determines both social and individual existence and awareness is the effect of economic conditions.   3. Social science and literature have the function of showing that present conditions can be changed.

After his early years of anarchism and expressionism and beginning at the time of his first encounter with Marxism, which occurred in 1923/24, Brecht was, in a sense, preoccupied with a single problem of stagecraft pedagogy: What can be done to prevent the spectator from losing himself passively in the figures and situations presented to him? What can be done to achieve that he maintains a critical distance from the events on the stage, that he understands those events to be a demonstration of a state of affairs which is as it is but which is not of necessity as it is, and that he will leave the theater as an individual determined to become engaged in the endeavor to effect a radical transformation of society?

In terms of literary history (and harking back to a time preceding the development of a "Marxist" aesthetics), the starting point and the initial basis of Brecht's dramaturgy was the movement known as the "new realism." In it we can recover the basic elements of Brecht's doctrine of the theater: the blasé—yet heroic, yet sentimental—demonstration of life "as it happens to be," the disruption of the spectator's empathy by the vaudeville trick of having the actor and his part break away each from the other, and an imminent social criticism which, it is true, had not yet been driven to the programmatic extreme of a black-and-white schematism. This was accomplished by Erwin Piscator whose antecedents were in the anti-art movement of Dadaism and who had tried immediately after the First World War to call into being a proletarian theater for the propagation of a social criticism of social-scientific orientation with the implication that it would call for political action. "The human individual of the stage," Piscator wrote, "has—as we see it—the significance of a social function. Neither his relationship to himself nor his relationship to God but his relationship to society constitutes our central concern. When he appears on the stage, the class or the social stratum that he represents appears with him. His conflicts—moral or spiritual or instinctual—are conflicts with society . . . the function of the revolutionary theater consists in taking reality as a starting point to potentiate social discrepancies into elements of accusation, of revolution, and of a new order." [39]

Like many others of his generation, Brecht underwent the natural and possibly unavoidable metamorphosis from expressionistic illuminism to hard-boiled realism. But he alone proved able to derive from the new matter-of-factness a dramatic theory and practice which raised the whole venture from the low low of political barkerdom and social satire to the level of high-class theater. Initially the literary Marxism of the twenties was little

more than an antibourgeois ideology that was in the air and
that lent itself nicely to fixing up the spontaneous forms of expression of a phase of development in the literary continuity with
a fitting ideological corset. Brecht alone exemplified the amalga-
mation of a spontaneous realism with the ex-post-facto rationale
of a handy ideology to form a system of aesthetics of his own
which in its turn exerted a feedback influence on his work as a
writer.

Surely, theories—in politics as well as in aesthetics—are not
wrong simply because they provide an a-posteriori explanation
and justification for things already extant. Furthermore, there
would be no reason to single out Brecht's aesthetics and to attrib-
ute to it a significance apart if its inventor had stated: This is the
kind of theater I propose to cultivate, pursuing by means of it a
specific purpose of political didacticism because I believe that it
has something to offer to my fellow men in the world of today.
But such modesty was not precisely characteristic of Brecht. He
preferred to claim that no doctrine of the theater other than his
deserved any kind of consideration; he claimed that he was writing for the public of tomorrow. And he never grew tired of point-
ing out what he considered an unseverable link between the only
possible, the only correct, that is, the Marxist interpretation of
history and the only possible, the only correct, that is, his conception of art.

It is of some interest in this connection to ask how the relationship between the political creed and the literary work presented itself in the case of writers who were drawn into the orbit
of national socialism or fascism. It was by no means as a lyrical
poet that Ezra Pound became a fascist but rather as a sectarian
of economic theory. Henry de Montherlant and Gottfried Benn
were drawn for a while into the current of fascism because they
thought they could find in it corroboration and possibly implementation of their élitistic vitalism of the chosen few. In none
of the three is there any immediate relationship between the
literary work and the political ideology in question. What strikes
us in Pound as well as in Montherlant and Benn is much rather
the incompatibility of a totalitarian and authoritarian system
with the extreme individualism of their several works and aesthe-

tic conceptions. In Brecht, by contrast, it is the political creed which carries the entire work and which permeates it, or which, at least, is claimed to carry and permeate the entire work. If we remove this substructure, that is, if we try to approach Brecht's work as though he had never uttered a single theorizing remark in reference to it, what we have left is the output of a highly gifted dramatist of the period of the Weimar republic whose plays— almost without exception and not barring those written at a later time—are dated by their dependence on that period and its atmosphere, endeavoring—all in all—to continue in a more or less modernized version the old theater of stock characters engaged in cloak-and-dagger ventures. We find ourselves confronted with a revival of the old drama of villains and heroes that throve through the impact of simple fables and simple figures on a public still able to derive edification and enjoyment from such a drastic simplification of the complexities of life. This kind of theater is fascinating and intriguing. It can be intelligent. When it breaks through the black-and-white schematism it shares by consanguinity with the vaudeville act—it does so, for instance, in *The Life of Galileo* and in *Mother Courage*—it comes close to ranking with the theater of the classics. But it never is modern theater. We can recognize in it the sixteenth, the seventeenth, the eighteenth, and the nineteenth centuries. We note that it revives basic forms of a classical theater of China and Japan. What we do not discern, because it is not there, is any kind of link to the thirties, forties, and fifties of the twentieth century whose crucial importance for the contemporary stage no one can deny. This shortcoming Brecht tried to make up for by hitching his playwright's wagon to the star of a supposedly progressivistic political ideology and by offering the promising explanation that his theater anticipated, as it were, the theater of the twenty-first century.

Brecht's crusade was aimed only on the face of it against the Aristotelian tradition of dramaturgy; his real butt was the individualistic and the psychological theater. He tried hard to give the impression that a basic prerequisite for a genuinely realistic and forward-looking literature was the careful and constantly conscious skirting of individualistic psychology. In point of fact, however, the collectivistic mode of presentation concerned with

social types and social roles rather than with individuals precedes
—both historically and genetically—the mode of presentation
in which the individual subject occupies the center of the stage.
Modern man, that is, post-medieval man, may well be characterized by reference to his ever stronger urge and ever growing ability
to relate whatever comes into his ken more intensely to his own
self. The social mobility of modern man, the possibility which is
potentially his of passing in the course of his life through many
classes, of playing many parts, and of living on many levels presupposes and demands that the individual be autonomous and
responsible to himself (regardless of the extent to which he may
succeed in fact in implementing his potential mobility).

Even if we agree—in keeping with the tenets of Marxist
theory—that what we call the personal life of the individual is
totally or primarily determined by external circumstances, it still
remains a fact that the individual has a personal life and must
cope with it. No one can postpone the solution of the problems
of his personal life until after the world revolution has removed
the (in this view) economically conditioned problems of his life.
This, however, implies for today and tomorrow, as it did for yesterday, that the primary function of art is not the demonstration
of the mutability of social circumstances but the presentation of
the conflicts which evolve for the individual from a given situation
and an accounting of the manner and means utilized by the
individual in his successful or failing endeavor to resolve his
conflicts. The hierarchy of values in which the theater of individualism and psychology ranks above the theater of society and
sociology derives its objective validity from the fact that the
individual human being as a concrete entity is alone the locus
where history and society can become manifest, can occur, can
be perceived in consciousness, can be experienced, lived, and suffered. Look at "society" from whatever angle you will: it remains
an abstraction devoid of a consciousness of its own, devoid of
feeling and sensation. When someone goes to see a play by Bertolt
Brecht—even a play by Bertolt Brecht—he is not a party cell or
work brigade but an individual with a brain of his own, a soul
of his own, a fate and destiny of his own, hoping to see explained
on the boards how what keeps him astir and what weighs heavily

on him did come about and how it can be dealt with. The failure
of the public in Brecht performances could never be accounted
for—as Ernst Schumacher tried to rationalize—by its habituation
to a falsely emotionalized "theater of the parasitic bourgeoisie"
but by the simple fact that ideological theses cannot be given
more than a semblance of palpable concreteness and that, above
all, they are hardly a substitute for the presentation of individually human conflicts. It is impossible not to refer at this point to
the by now characteristically familiar detail that the device which
Brecht had adopted for himself and which he liked to display in
the form of an ostentatious poster in his room was: "Truth is
concrete." [40] It is strange that this snappy aphorism served Brecht
only to excuse himself from the contemplation of the really concrete truths of human life. Compared to the palpable concreteness
of individual spiritual and physical ills and joys, all merely social
problems—regardless of whether we wish to interpret them in
bourgeois or proletarian terms—are extremely abstract (and secondary in etiology).

When one postulates that the true function of the theater is
a matter of political didacticism—and this Brecht did postulate
—one cheats the public out of the realization that an understanding of the social genesis of the individual's present condition
(which may—if backed by critical acuity—arouse the will to
bring about a social change) cannot by that token contribute in
the least to a solution of the problems with which the individual
has to cope here and now, that is to say, long before the mutability
of any externally social factors entering into his situation can become evident. Didactic moralities and vaudeville acts, cloak-and-
dagger dramas and social satire have all their meaningful functions. And why should it be wrong to harness the theater to the
bandwagon of a political or a philosophical or a scientific idea?
And why should it not be possible to be good or to be had at put-
ting the theater to such uses? But the slogan that the essence of
history is class struggle is no substitute for the old truth that the
struggles which do lead to decisions are those which the individual
human being fights out within himself and with himself. It is possible to assume that Brecht was seriously of the opinion that his
"fruit pickers" and "motor-vehicle construction engineers" would

welcome it as "gay" entertainment if the theater supplied them
with instructions on how to prune an apple tree or to install motors
with due regard for the repairman's future troubles? Or are we to
conclude from the proclamation of the antipsychological theater
(and its claim to exclusivity) that the proper task of the progressive drama is to deceive men as to the individual character of
their destiny?

Theories to Be Supplied Later

During the years of his Scandinavian exile (1933 to 1941),
Brecht—as various notes jotted down by him at the time indicate
—was ready to correct his theory that it is the function of the epic
theater to prevent every kind of identification and empathy. He
now insisted on nothing more radical than that the empathy
should be of the "right" kind. On January 12, 1941, he wrote in
his diary: "We should never forget in considering these things
that non-Aristotelian theater is first of all a form of *Theater*. It
serves specific social objectives and has no ambitions of usurpation relative to the theater in general. It is quite possible for me
to utilize in certain performances Aristotelian theater by the side
of its non-Aristotelian counterpart. In performing now *Saint Joan
of the Stockyards*, for instance, it might be advantageous to effect
on occasion an attitude of empathy toward Saint Joan (from today's point of view, that is), for this figure undergoes a process
of increasing awareness so that empathy on the part of the spectator may very well result from this angle in a clearer survey of
the major continuities." [41]
It appears thus that two points need to be considered in this
connection. On the one hand, Brecht declared, against the background of his prior dramatic and aesthetic theories, that his
Galileo was "opportunistic" (diary entry of February 23, 1939),
which doubtless referred not only to the Aristotelian technique
but also to the overall design of the play as a drama of character.
On the other hand, he now presented a theoretical justification
of the mixed form which meanwhile had evolved. From the fact

that Brecht had condemned all "empathy" in a lecture "on the experimental theater" presented to the students of the University of Stockholm as recently as May 1939—that is, when the *Galileo* had just been completed—it is clear that he looked "after the fact" for the theoretical justification of what he felt urged to write, and that his plays are not systematic exemplifications of previously worked-out recipes. Just as in the case of *Galileo* the "opportunistic" play was there first and was followed by the theory of opportunism, so the vaudeville plays and the didactic plays as types and genres had come into being before Brecht supplied the corresponding theory of the epic theater, of the non-Aristotelian drama, and the alienation effect. He himself wrote, "When I read *Das Kapital* by Marx, I understood my plays," [42] and Martin Esslin judged that Brecht "evolved his theories on the aesthetics of the stage as rational commentaries to account—a posteriori—for the modifications to which his taste, his style, and his theatrical practice were subject." [43]

It is in particular *The Life of Galileo* that testifies to the unhappy influence exerted by Brecht's ideological obsession on the character and the quality of his works. This is so because the original version of the play marked the point in Brecht's career when he was least a theoretician and most a pure dramatist. What Brecht was ultimately trying to do was to reshape a fully differentiated historical character drama in order to make of it once again a piece of simplistic politburo propaganda. It is fortunate that he was not completely successful in this venture, but a critical review of his revisions does force us to conclude that the graftings of socialist ethics and aesthetics harm in decisive respects the convincing impact and hence the literary quality of the work while doing violence to the historical truth. The *Galileo* is the only play in which Brecht used as his theme the documented destinies of a great historical figure. What he set out to present was clearly delineated in terms of subject matter by universally known or accessible documentation, implying that the plan to write a play on Galileo could appeal to Brecht only during a phase of his career when his theorizing and politicizing propensities were of minor significance. This—as we have pointed out before—held true during Brecht's years in Denmark. With these antecedents it appears

as a matter of necessity that his subsequent attempt to recast his
Galileo in an ideological mold resulted in total failure. The character and the guilt of Galileo can only be approached in terms of
individualism and on a psychological basis. His actions and reac-
tions were a matter which he had to settle with himself alone
precisely because the political and social conditions prevailing
at the time did not permit any other manner of acting and reacting. This is why the contrivedly constructed "social crime" of
Galileo produces no dramatic tension whatsoever. The dramatic
tension which does pervade the play is produced—even in the
final version—through Galileo's clash with the Church and
through his complexly individual character which no one—not
even Brecht—could reduce by force to a black-and-white schematism. Galileo was not—as Brecht so desperately wanted him to
be—on the one hand a hero and on the other a criminal; he was
neither the one nor the other. The character traits which Brecht
at the time of the Berlin rehearsals tried so hard to move poles
apart are closely adjacent and, indeed, interfused features of an
entirely healthy and normal character not only in the historical
Galileo but also in the Galileo of the Danish version of Brecht's
play. Galileo was neither a moral genius nor an immoral one. He
was a scientific genius. In the realignment of the second version
and even in the extreme tendentiousness of the Berlin presentation, Galileo comes out as a human individual reacting the way
human individuals will reasonably and understandably react in
such situations. He does not come out as an abhorrent monster
on trial before the court of justice of world history.

   The Life of Galileo shares the great possibilities of the dramatist Brecht, and it shows the limits which this potentially great
dramatist imposed upon himself. What reduced Brecht to the
status of a second-rate dramatist is the fact that he did not allow
the figures created by him to have an individual destiny of their
own but made of them products and objects of external problems.
Brecht insisted on doing away with the identity of his figures with
themselves, with the identity of the actor with his part, with the
identity of the dramatist with his play. Since *The Life of Galileo*
proved more recalcitrant than any of Brecht's other plays to his
efforts to make it conform to his demands, it represented more

than any other a challenge to his dramatic and aesthetic theorizing. During the Berlin rehearsals Brecht time and again felt the
urge to discuss fundamental aspects of his theatrical doctrines.
Käthe Rülicke reports: "Thus it is not the 'character' of Galileo
that deserves our interest but the social demeanor of Galileo. As
Brecht put it on one occasion during the rehearsals: 'It is not
interesting that a human individual fights with himself; what is
interesting is that he fights with others.' In fact, during the rehearsals Brecht almost never discussed the character of a figure
but its type of behavior. He almost never explained what a person
said but rather what he did. And when a statement of Brecht's
concerned some characteristic trait of a figure, he did not derive that trait from a psychological but from a social complex.
He showed the character of a figure through the mode of its
behavior." [44]

And a few pages later on: "Brecht considered all idealist
dramas, including Goethe's, to be playable only in a critical presentation, for: 'The word of the poet is not more sacred than it
is true. The theater is not the servant of the poet but of society.'
In Brecht's view, what can interest us—regardless of how the plays
were written—are not the conflicts of Faust, Macbeth, Hamlet,
Lear, Coriolanus, Othello with themselves but the social conditions that led them to experience those conflicts. And how else
can social conditions be shown nowadays if not from the point of
view of historical materialism, with the methods of materialistic
dialects, as class struggles, that is to say critically?" [45]

If it were not Brecht of whom Frau Rülicke reports these
pearls of wisdom and if Brecht were not enjoying both in the
West and in the East the privileges of the sort of diplomatic immunity that is enjoyed by two-legged national shrines, the whole
question would long since have been filed away with the notation
that there is universal agreement regarding the fact that a subtle
way of processing Marxist doctrines and theoretical thinking is
not precisely the strength of this man. Imagine, if you will, the
insipidity or ludicrousness of a socialistically staged Shakespeare,
with the conflicts of Macbeth, Hamlet, and Lear presented as the
effect of the struggle of the classes. As for the statement that the
theater should not be the servant of the poet but of society, it is

this sort of think one would expect to find in the entertainment section of *Neues Deutschland* but not in the verbatim records of Brecht rehearsals. What "idealistic" poet has ever had the objective of making the theater his "servant"? Is there one who would not have endorsed the statement as applicable to his own production that the word of the poet is not more sacred than it is true? Even reflections which seem sound at first blush cannot withstand a closer scrutiny. If Brecht wrote, for instance (in the "Small Organon"), "For from what goes on between human beings they derive all that is subject to discussion, criticism, modification," we may be inclined to accept uncritically the validity of the statement presented—as it is—in a tone of patriarchic wisdom. But, as we look more closely, we again find nothing left but the shallowest kind of ideological rhetoric. It is the little word "all" that makes the statement both vacuous and untrue. Even a a Marxist ought to be able to see that it is possible to discuss what goes on inside a human being, such as for instance the conflict of conscience of a Galileo.

Brecht did not reason on the basis of experience but under the aegis of a predetermined political doctrine. His acuity of vision was excellent for specific situations, but he was virtually incapable of thinking systematically, that is to say, of establishing (without the premature introduction of a ready-made answer) the connection between honest experience and honest deduction that alone can support the soundness of a theory. What Brecht called his theories were on the whole very superficial and mechanical attempts to apply a simplistic Marxism to the dramatic structure of the pre-existing vaudeville theater of types.

During his final years Brecht did on occasion make utterances which seemed to suggest that he realized—at least at that time—the weakness of his speculations. In "Conversation During a Rehearsal" (1953) he remarked that his theoretical observations had been taken too absolutely: "All my theories are much more naive than is generally assumed, than my way of expressing myself may seem to indicate . . . I believe the trouble began because my plays had to be performed correctly if they were to be effective, and so I had to describe for a non-Aristotelian drama —O sadness!—an epic theater—O misery!" [47]

The Case of Bertolt Brecht Brooks
No Explanation Other than a Psychological One

If then—as Brecht himself confirmed toward the end of his
life—the theories were supplied after the fact, we cannot but
wonder why a man who was everything rather than a theoretician
should have begun to theorize at all and why it was Marxism that
was made to supply the structural skeleton for his speculations.
Or, to reformulate the question in more general terms, why was
it that one of the most promising dramatic talents produced by
Germany in the course of the past fifty years could not rid himself
of a political and aesthetic ideology that made his entire production wind up in a blind alley?

We must emphasize at this point that in asking the foregoing
question we claim to be doing so on the basis of objectively veri-
fiable facts, implying that we reject the notion that our evaluation
of Brecht is a matter of subjective taste. The realization of the
priority of individual to social problems does not simply differ-
entiate between two equally valid and worthy views of life and
of art, it draws a line between a more mature and less mature,
between a more sophisticated and a less sophisticated awareness
of existence. That man is mature who understands his fate to be
a personal fate (regardless of what powers may have molded it),
who accepts his fate in that sense and endeavors to impart to it a
commensurate form (because it is clear to him that this subjective
task cannot be turned over to the care of a collective doctrine and
an anonymous authority), and who projects the inner conditions
of his existence into the public domain in precisely the way in
which he projects the external conditions of his existence from
the public to the innermost private domain, welding these two
spheres of his life into the integral entity we are accustomed to
calling a "personality."

The "main task of the theater" is by no means "the interpretation of the fable and its transmittal by an appropriate process
of alienation" but the interpretation of the processes which the
events of the fable precipitate within the individual human being.
Surely, it is important to change the world, that is, to improve it,
but this important assignment will not spare us the necessity of

passing muster and of coping from birth to death with the world
as we find it. An art and a literature that are silent on these scores,
that refuse to help us in these concerns are of low moral and low
aesthetic ranks. "Today," Brecht wrote, "when the 'free' individual personality has come to be a hindrance in the further
deployment of the potentialities of human production, the em-
pathy-oriented techniques of art have lost their justification. The
individual human subject must delegate his functions to the great
collective, which is a process involving desperate struggles as it
goes on before our very eyes." [48]

If this passage led up to the conclusion that the creative
achievement of the individual human being plays a progressively
receding role in research and technology by reason of the ever-
increasing importance of teamwork, it might indeed be felt to
make sense; as the guiding principle for a new theory of the
drama it is sheer nonsense. It appears that Brecht never understood (or refused to understand) that in the middle of the
twentieth century nonpsychological theater can only be metapsychological and not unpsychological. Ionesco, who is one of the
most important representatives of the dramatic conception that
goes beyond the conventional psychologistic approach not by
rejecting but by sublimating it, has managed to state in three short
sentences all that needs to be said in this matter: "We all are a
part of a historical continuity and pertain to a particular historical
moment. But this historical moment is far from claiming us completely. On the contrary, it expresses only the unessential part
of us." [49]

Psychological literature is a higher form (in an evolutionary
sense) because it provides a more differentiated image of man and
because it has understood that man can and must bring into being,
at this very moment and at any moment, a "classless society." A
socialistic literature in which the individual is not merely placed
in society but replaced by it is lower and inferior because it draws
a simplistic and hence a false picture of man.

There is but one approach to the solution of the enigma
Brecht—the one he expressly rejected for his political and literary program: the psychological approach. Brecht's seemingly
insuperable urge to theorize must have had its base in the urgent

desire to have his literary productions appear to be not the expression of subjective emotions and convictions but the result of objective calculations.[50] "Whoever it is whom you strive to find, I am not he." The fact that Brecht started out on this flight into objectivity very early in life and that he persisted in it to the end suggests an underlying mechanism involving an extraordinarily marked and seemingly irreversible warping of his mind.

Brecht was the prototype of a psychological communist and was, for that very reason, more firmly and more fatefully bound to that doctrine than could ever hold true of a Marxist by conviction. The only element of "objective" conviction in Brecht's confession of faith in Marx and Lenin was the humanitarian idea, the indignation in the face of all the wrong in the world. The rest was rationalization on the basis of a personal problem. In the last analysis, every theory—be it religious, be it philosophical, or be it aesthetic—may be viewed as a characteristic expression of those embracing it. This is so quite apart from the question as to whether the theory is right or wrong. What is decisive with respect to the expressive value and also the truth value of the conviction a man holds, is whether he proclaims ideas which adequately express his ego and his problem permitting both to come to the fore or whether he aligns himself with an ideology that will serve to hide his ego and his problem. A man either will seek to establish full identity with what he is or he will flee this identity and strive to repress an essential portion of his subjectivity.

The anti-individualism and antipsychologism parading in the garb of the communist faith is so clearly a classical exemplification of the ideology of repression and concealment that it is bound to appear someday in some manual of depth psychology. The fact that Brecht kept repeating ad nauseum that what was crucially important in life and on the stage was the behavior of the human individual, that is, his social function, and the parallel fact that he formulated in his aesthetics the demand that the actor must not identify himself with his part and that the spectator must not identify himself with the figures on stage can only be taken to signify: I, Bertolt Brecht, do not want you to be concerned with my person, with my private life, with my subjectivity; I am, as far as you are concerned, the Marxist playwright and school-

master, the stage communist, the man with the spare-me-the-brush
haircut and the proletarian jacket. In that pose you may judge
me and evaluate me, and look, I can even set you up with the
necessary ideological measuring sticks.—Ever since Brecht had
become a public figure—that is to say, at the latest after the
success of the *Threepenny Opera*—he never tired of keeping up
this pose and of impressing upon others that this was his style.
"Your method is too much method," says Volumnia to the "Chief"
in Günter Grass's *The Plebeians Are Rehearsing Their Uprising*.

Throughout his life, beginning with the way he set up his
room in his paternal home in Augsburg—with a skull, the Tristan
score, a picture of the god Baal, and the "twelve suras for my
visitors"—and continuing to the end when he worked out in great
detail directives as to the material for the coffin in which he
wished to be buried, the inscription on his grave, and the manner
in which his burial was to be carried out, Brecht was preoccupied
with molding his presence in the Brecht matrix designed by him
at a very early time. He was a snob and a mannerist of the purest
water; he was a sort of Stefan George in work clothes. He cultivated inelegance and drab sobriety with as much pretense as
others do exquisite refinement. And it was the function of all
these ideological, habitual, and decorative utensils to build up
a public Brecht image of such strikingly clear contours that no
one would as much as suspect the existence, in back of it or underneath it, of an original B. B. with differing characteristics. In this
"Building a Part," communism played the decisive role, for its
function—of the utmost gravity and replete with far-reaching
implications—was, so to speak, to camouflage the camouflage.
Since Stalin, it was—to say the least—unusual that snobbism was
the motive inducing anyone to become a partisan of the dictator-
ship of the proletariat. In Brecht, this unusual event came to pass.
After the storm-and-stress twenties with their romantic socialism
and parlor bolshevism, Brecht did not divest himself of communism but in fact made of it a fashion design of his own. Communism provided him with the ideal setting for continuing—with
other means—his flight from his identity. The contrived confession of faith in a radically objectivistic and collectivistic doctrine
made it possible for him to elude forever the demands which to

the adult human being are inherent in the process of maturation of one's personality. Thus a biographical liability came to represent in Brecht's case a programmatic asset. Throughout his life Brecht remained arrested on the specific level of problems of post-puberty and pre-adulthood.

The psychoanalyst Eric Erikson has explicitly discussed the phenomena of the "crisis of identity" which he defines as follows: "It stands to reason that late adolescence is the most favorable period, and late adolescent personalities of any age group the best subjects, for indoctrination; because in adolescence an ideological realignment is by necessity in process and a number of ideological possibilities are waiting to be hierarchically ordered by opportunity, leadership, and friendship. Any leadership, however, must have the power to encase the individual in a spatial arrangement and in a temporal routine which at the same time narrow down the sensory supply from the world and block his sexual and aggressive drives, so that a new needfulness will eagerly attach itself to a new world-image. At no other time as much as in adolescence does the individual feel so exposed to anarchic manifestations of his drives; at no other time does he so need oversystematized thoughts and overvalued words to give a semblance of order to his inner world. He therefore is willing to accept ascetic restrictions which go counter to what he would do if he were alone—faced with himself, his body, his musings—or in the company of old friends; he will accept the *sine qua non* of indoctrination, lack of privacy. (The Church could never have become an ideological institution on the basis of hermitism.) Needless to say, good and evil must be clearly defined as forces existing from all beginning and perseverating into all future; therefore all memory of the past must be starved or minutely guided, and all intention focused on the common utopia. No idle talk can be permitted. Talk must always count, count for or against one's readiness to embrace the new ideology totally—to the point of meaning it. In fact, the right talk, the vigorous song, and the radical confession in public must be cultivated." [51]

It is to be hoped that someday a psychological study of Bertolt Brecht as a young man will be undertaken and published. The passage just quoted could be taken over into it virtually un-

changed. It is in such a study—in its absence, in the material for
one and not in politico-logical or aesthetic considerations—that
we must look for the key that can resolve the problem of the case
of Bertolt Brecht. One important shift, however, needs to be introduced into the emotional state described by Erikson. Brecht
persevered in his juvenile fixation to authoritarian ideology because at the precise moment when it ceased to be an undoubtedly
genuinely experienced self-evident truth and began to be a calcu-
lated and external template of existence, it made possible the very
thing whose prevention had originally been its function: the acting out or rather the living out of the "sexual and aggressive
drives," the freeing of "the body and its dreams" in the private
sphere, which is hidden to the probing eye of the public. For him
who realizes that he does not have what it takes to be an ascetic
and who does not simultaneously develop the ability to transform
the "unbridled manifestations of his urges" into a socially accept-
able subjective form, the determined adherence to a collectivistic
ideology represents indeed an ideal pattern of life. An individual
in this situation gives to the ideology what the ideology demands,
that is to say, the unqualified right to determine the social role,
while he himself acquires in exchange the right to live out whatever he feels urged to live out in a realm which, to the ideology,
is quasi-nonexistent.

As could have been expected, Brecht endeavored with great
care to screen off his "intimate sphere" against all scrutinizing
glances. We know but little about the circumstances of his private
life. In the Brecht biography in pictures prepared by Kurt Fassmann we are told that Brecht's father was "a stern head of the
family who demanded respect." The son Bertolt felt so greatly
drawn to his mother that we need not fear we are distorting the
facts with a psychoanalytical bias when we claim to discern evidence of a pronounced maternal attachment of lifelong persistence. In Brecht's works the figure of the mother appears again
and again, and in his life a woman came to occupy the central
position who had much of the mother and little of a mistress:
Helene Weigel. The situation is thus classically that of the Oedi-
pus complex: the longing to replace the father in the favors of
the mother and to achieve simultaneously identification with the

father; the longing to come into sole possession of the mother and simultaneously the fear of being punished by the father for this longing. The solution of the dilemma was attained through a pronounced external identification with a paternal world that permitted simultaneously the secret internal identification with the maternal world. This simple basic pattern (the genesis and underlying mechanisms of which would require for their elucidation much more detailed information about Brecht's early years than is available to us) persisted in Brecht's life as a fixation of unusual strength. In order to be able to simultaneously "live out" and conceal his subjectivity, he was ready to pay the high price of the sacrifice of his individuality at the altar of a system that took no interest in his private sins but also left him without any possibility of self-realization in a sense implying an individually idiosyncratic impact in the public and social spheres. Brecht's submission under the authoritarian doctrine of communism involved no doubt traits of a compulsive neurosis, that is, of a self-inflicted punishment for his undercover subjectivism which he felt to be sinful.

The artistic development of Brecht reflects likewise in its stages the ontogenetic phases of human growth up to the level of adolescence. The first stage represents a repetition of the attempt of the infant to take possession of the world. "That, too," wrote Arnold Bronnen in his recollections of the time of his friendship with Brecht during the years from 1921 to 1923, "he had in common with a child: Whatever he saw, whatever he heard about, he wanted to own." [52]

In *Baal*, in *Drums in the Night*, and in *In the Jungle of Cities*, the world of realities is the booty of the I, the object of the I's orgastic lust, which it wants to have and to devour in its entirety. The play, *In the Jungle of Cities*, which was performed for the first time in 1923—the very year in which Brecht met Helene Weigel and began to concern himself with Marxism—ends with the statement: "The chaos has been used up. It was the best of times." The best of times reached its end because reality proved to be immune to being devoured and had to be coped with in some other way. This problem Brecht solved henceforth in three ways: by adaptation, by rebellion, and by trickery. To exemplify, first, by adaptation: The bourgeois capitalist world is accepted as a brute fact (as for instance in the *Threepenny Opera*). Second, by rebellion: The bourgeois capitalist disorder is rejected pending the revaluation of all its values (as for example in *Measures Taken*). Third, by trickery: The chaos (by no means used up) is removed both from the real and from the utopian object world and granted asylum in the realm of private subjectivity (as for instance in Brecht's lyrical poems). All this can be achieved to the satisfaction of a "Jesuit of the here below" (Max Frisch) by carrying through life, held high like a banner, that basic bit of Marxistic wisdom which avers that man is nothing but "the sum total of the conditions of society."

Brecht's pattern of life was in theory rigorous and doctrinaire, in practice either cynical and opportunistic or sentimental and subjectivistic, the first in its extrovert and the second in its introvert orientation. To be sure, these three spheres and elements were not always neatly separated from each other but entered instead into the most varied combinations. There are lyrical tones echoing through the ideological expostulations; an element of trickery and sarcasm reverberates through Brecht's most intimate privacy; and in his struggles with the practices of the bourgeois capitalist world, Brecht on occasion derived genuine pleasure from the fact that he mastered the skills needed to get along in that sphere. All in all, however, it would seem that few others before and after Brecht succeeded as well as he did in preventing a more thorough fusion of those various areas from occurring.

The endeavor to trace the simple yet complex pattern of Brecht's life can lead to the discovery of fertile perspectives only if the fact is never lost sight of that the behavioral peculiarities described did not arise as the result of rational planning but came about as the necessary product of psychological mechanisms, representing the "must-do" solution of an individual who never acquired what is needed to cross the threshold leading to maturity. This later stage—that of maturity—is characterized precisely by the accomplished balance of subject and object references, of reality and ideality. The world, as one finds it, is not allowed to exert its demonic impact, it is not accepted in its inadequacy, but it is understood as an assignment, as a task. Utopian dreams are brought down to a level where reality can touch them, and the libido is not concealed but given validity through projection into the public and social realm. This building up, not of a part, but of a person has one fundamental prerequisite: that the individual must have overcome his fear of his own instinctual needs, that he must have accomplished the identification of the id and the ego, permitting in due course the inclusion of the superego in his total identity. What Brecht apparently was unable to evolve, what marked the point where he failed, was the ability to accept and own up to, without self-consciousness, his sexual and aggressive drive, that is to say "his body and its dreams."

There is only one area of expression in which Brecht permitted his emotions the freedom of spontaneity. This is the area of lyrical poetry. ("My lyrical poems are private in character.") Here we find time and again his subjectivity breaking out from the prison of his intimate life. Brecht's poetic production includes several of the most beautiful German love poems, but he always tried to belittle his contribution as a "versifier," insisting that it was worthless compared to what he had to offer as a playwright. And—characteristically—in none of his plays is there a successful presentation of a love relationship.

Fritz Sternberg wrote in his *Recollections of Bertolt Brecht* that Brecht confessed to him during one of their encounters in the winter of 1926/27 that after *Drums in the Night* he had found it impossible to portray a pair of lovers: "Since the time when I wrote this play it has no longer been possible for me to derive from the relationship of a man to a woman a vision strong enough to carry an entire drama." [53]

Drums in the Night was written in 1922. In the same year Brecht married Marianne Zoff, from whom he was divorced in 1927. Late in 1923 he and Helene Weigel met. Brecht's most beautiful love poem, "Memory of Maria A.," was printed for the first time in 1926. Comparatively little is known about Brecht's relations to women. To be sure, throughout his life he was surrounded by female collaborators who were, as it were, members of the family. During his Scandinavian years, there were Margarete Steffin and Ruth Berlau, both of whom were to accompany him to America. Margarete Steffin had to stay behind in Moscow be-

cause of a pulmonary ailment. She died there shortly after
Brecht's departure. In Hollywood, in 1946, Brecht's ménage and
Ruth Berlau were rejoined by Elisabeth Hauptmann, who had
been Brecht's closest collaborator during his years in Berlin.

In this connection we may well raise the question as to why
Brecht's first version of *Galileo*—which on the whole, respected
the facts of history—did not assign the role of his keeper and
guardian to Galileo's son Vincenzo (who, in fact, did have that
function) but to his daughter Virginia and as to why Brecht in
the final version of the play redrew Virginia's character entirely
in negative terms. Since women who are convinced of the validity
of an "idea" are apt to be particularly fanatic about it, the possibility suggested itself that highly personal experiences of
Brecht's supplied the ultimate motivation in these events. What
is involved here may well be the ambivalence of a psyche seeking
maternal safety in love, while it sensed at all times the necessity
of being on its guard against the prying scrutiny of a mistress with
a sufficiently strong political commitment to enable her to play
the role of informer.

Brecht's preoccupation with the problem of homosexuality
is reflected in several of his plays, that is, in *Baal*, in *In the Jungle
of Cities*, and in *Edward II*. In two other plays—*Man is Man* and
Private Tutor—acts of self-emasculation are committed. Such acts,
to put it mildly, are uncommon in stage plays. The significance of
these miscellaneous data must not be exaggerated, but they do
permit the inference that the libidinous urges and responses of
Brecht were of a kind inducing him to keep them cautiously concealed. It is in this need for repression that we may look for the
roots of Brecht's exaggeratedly violent rejection of all forms of
"psychologism" in favor of a function for man that is exclusively
social and thoroughly pre-cleansed of every last vestige of chaos.
Brecht's inability—acknowledged by the best-informed witness,
that is, by Brecht himself—to present on the stage a man and a
woman in love reflects a trauma that went far beyond the repression of a purely sexual "disorder" and involved the entire range
of psycho-erotic strata of the ego. To be sure, a love story can be
presented without any kind of reference to sexual problems, but
it cannot be imagined without an interest in what is going on

inside the individuals concerned. The attitude of sober sophistica-
tion in contemplating his own role in all situations in life—assumed by Brecht at a very early time, as early, in fact, as his
expressionist period, though with a transition which it is impossible to date precisely—prevented, from the very beginning, the
development in the actor, that is, in Brecht, of that modicum of
subjectivity and empathetic identification without which a genuine emotion simply cannot be presented. What can be achieved
with such dramaturgic devices is only the typical attitude of
"the male of the species" who is afraid of having and of showing
emotions and therefore belittles his experiences of love by an
ostentatious display of irony.

Every love relationship which amounts to more than a response to sex hormones in some bedroom with carefully closed
curtains lays claim to some area in the public and social domain.
It places the pair of lovers in contrast to society in that it detracts
from their availability for the fulfillment of social functions. A
relationship which transcends and lasts beyond the mere sexual
act, that is, a relationship characterized by a spiritual involvement of the psyche, results for the individual not only in a loosening of his ties to the family but also in a similar loosening of his
ties to the "fellows" or "brothers" and "sisters" or "comrades"
or "colleagues" of other groups in life or at work. It is for this
reason that all rigorous communal ideologies endeavor to reduce
the role of the eros to its purely sexual manifestations. When this
is accomplished, the individual is unavailable for social requirements only for the duration of the coitus from which he emerges
"socially unscathed." The basis of what we call "personality" is
most probably the specific energy and the specific behavioral
mode which the individual must evolve in order to protect his
relationship to one particular "you" against the usurpation of
society.

Alexander Mitscherlich has given us a succinct formulation
covering this problem: "Mature, that is, personally cultured, is
not he who loves mankind, who loves the party or some other
abstraction, not he who loves the Holy Virgin or some other numi-
nous entity but he who has achieved the ability to love another
human being throughout and through all the tensions of ambi-

valent experience that may enter into and sustain such a relationship." [54]

This consummation of a love relationship in all its occult and all its patent dimensions is nowhere to be found in Brecht. What we do find in his dramas are only successful representations of women who are intrinsically mothers: Pelagea Wlassowa in *The Mother*, Johanna Dark in *Saint Joan of the Stockyards*, Teresa Carrar in *Señora Carrar's Rifles*, Anna Fierling in *Mother Courage*. Even prostitutes and women of the demimonde do not, insofar as their characterization involves positive traits, deploy the virtues of women in love but of women who are mothers: Leocadia Begbick in *The Rise and Fall of the Town of Mahagonny* and *Man is Man*, Shen Te in *The Good Woman of Setzuan*.

What we find in Brecht is, then, the positive relationship to the safety and anonymity of the world of the mother; what we do not find is the personal relationship to the opposite sex, the I-you relationship which presupposes a balance of taking and giving, of self-abandonment and self-assertion, of imposing one's own individuality and recognizing the individuality of another, that is to say, a relationship the development of which is organically and naturally impossible while the individual is still in the phase of the crisis of the subject's identity. In Brecht this latter phase has become a permanent condition. Its most characteristic trait—the break between a concealed libido which is simultaneously experienced as lust and as sin, the break between a father world which is sensed to be corrupt and an antipodal world of exacting ideals—appears in Brecht in arrested permanence. In lieu of the phenomenon of a spontaneous integration in the form of an I that is ready and able to say yes to itself, there appears the phenomenon of a forced integration through the submission of the ego to a superego.

The more it is the individual's endeavor to repress his drives or the more he feels himself to be at the mercy of his drives, the more rigorous must be the principle of order that can be expected to ban the anarchy of the libido at least from the public and social areas of life. In Brecht we observe how a youthful propensity for anti-individualistic moralizing becomes solidified as the structural skeleton of his philosophy of life and how the materials making up his philosophy of life are supplied from the reservoir —fortuitously accessible through historical and personal circumstances—of Marxism. The ideology of Marxism offers a neatly circumscribed doctrine of salvation which is easily reduced to a few simple formulas of black-and-white applicability, providing —above all—the possibility for the individual to side with all that is good and progressive by a simple profession of faith. The individual, as a subject, can now regard himself as absolved, for the basic convictions which he has endorsed include the principle that it is utterly meaningless to attempt to find individual solutions for individual problems. In fact, there are no individual problems, that is to say, problems felt to be such are in fact social problems which can be resolved only through a radical change in the conditions of the external world. The utopian faith in the system of a totally whole and hale world justifies every kind of personal failure in the real world (short of disobedience toward the system), for it is not more than an elementary matter of cause and effect that untoward conditions will lead of necessity to the development of dubious subjects.

In *The Measures Taken*, the play (written in 1930) in which Brecht formulated this anti-ethics most uncompromisingly, we find the passage: "Fighting for communism demands that one is able to fight and to not fight; to speak the truth and to not speak the truth; to serve and to refuse service; to keep promises and not to keep promises; to face dangers and to skirt them; to be recognized and to be unrecognizable. Fighting for communism means that of all virtues one has but one: that one is fighting for communism."

Brecht had in him enough of the sprite of provocation to note (and to mention) implications inherent in such a system which the functionaries of it either fail to see or in any event prefer not to speak about. In the psychological communism of Brecht—precisely because it was psychological and not logical— there was a great deal of aggressiveness even against communism itself. Time and again Brecht pushed his thinking about the system all the way to the limit beyond which the break occurs that makes it appear absurd. But only once or twice—before the world and before himself—did Brecht dare take the fateful step beyond.

A case in point is, for instance, Brecht's famous epilogue to the events of the Seventeenth of June of the Year 1953 in which he wrote: "Would it not then be simpler for the government to dissolve the people and elect another?" A man who is able to see this point, to put it down in writing, and who yet remains a communist, is not a communist by reflection and conclusion but is bound to communism by psychological compulsion. Brecht's anti-individualism was dishonest, it was "phony," for it was proclaimed by Brecht as a deceptive façade which he needed in order—in back of it—not to repress his subjective drives but to indulge them in concealed privacy. In other words, his anti-individualism was dishonest because it never occurred to him that for its sake he might have to sacrifice his private ego on the altar of socialist world salvation. Brecht was a "Tutor" who did not wish to be emasculated and therefore displayed exaggerated eagerness in the pursuit of his teaching duties.

In his book, *My Twentieth Century*, Ludwig Marcuse wrote: "What matters to Brecht is to save face and 'to have the last word' for the record. Underneath he is humane and amiable." [55]

Brecht was obsessed by the fear of social failure, the fear of a compromising public exposure. This arrogant adept at literary provocation manifested in his dealings with any kind of official authority a truly ludicrous dread of being censured and of being liable to penalty. He was the born nonhero.[56] Both in the West and in the East his arsenal of ideological weapons never included open contradiction but consisted primarily of stratagems and irony. He never took a stand and never left himself open. He knew how to avoid head-on collisions. Dissemblance was his element of life—a pellucid style of maneuvering under a system whose right to demand obedience he fully acknowledged while keeping it sufficiently at arm's length to assure his private desires complete gratification. By establishing publicly his identification with an authoritarian principle of order he obtained the concession of a materially secure life in a collectivistic order of society with all-inclusive rules and regulations and yet enjoyed the privilege of absolute immunity in a private sanctuary providing the possibility of indulging and gratifying all his subjective wishes and drives.

Under such conditions, a "privatistic" sort of character is bound to evolve whose field of dynamics is restricted to a hermetically sealed realm within, that is, a character deprived of that one function through which alone subjectivity matures into personality: projection into the world, into the social and societal arena where it must be maintained and answered for in the encounter with other individualities. What is guaranteed in the constitutions of free democratic countries under the term of basic human rights is precisely this sphere of the spontaneous and unencumbered deployment of the most varied human subjects. To be sure, nothing is more superfluous than the freedom of speech, the freedom of opinion, the freedom of worship, the freedom of aesthetic decision and of scientific research, if one is satisfied with deploying and employing one's needs and talents within the four walls of one's private home. The whims a man has as a husband or father, the way he eats, sleeps, and loves are not subject to state control even under the most totalitarian system. Indeed, in this area safety valves are allowed and provided to give vent to pent-up resentment and aggressiveness, and modes of behavior that are at odds with the official code of morals are overlooked. This implies that under a social system which assigns to the state, its rules and ideology, the title of possession in the domain of the basic rights of the human personality, the danger is extraordinarily great that demoralization should affect and pervade the private world in which alone subjectivity has a chance to unfold.

On the other hand, any kind of authoritarian social order offers the ideal solution for the problems of life of men and women whose psychological constitution requires a clear-cut separation of the two realms of subjective secrecy and indulgence and objective performance of a public role. Through the profession of faith in such a system, a weakness—as though by a sleight of hand—becomes a strength. There ensues, indeed, for the one involved the possibility of experiencing a feeling of superiority relative to the world of "unprincipled" individualism. In this perspective, psychological communism provides the individual simultaneously with the possibility of taking revenge on reality which he himself proved unable to master, for that reality is now thoroughly mastered by the system with which the individual

professes identity. Here lies the root of the great attraction which
all authoritarian systems have for immature subjects and for those
who have failed in their lives. Such individuals are relieved of the
need for coping with life the moment they identify themselves
with the system and profess to be exclusively its functionaries or
the executors of its dictates. The less a social order regulates the
thought and the demeanor of the individual, the greater are the
demands which it makes on the individual's potentiality of creation, his power of decision, and his sense of responsibility. He is
obliged to impart shape and form not only to his private life,
which no outsider can observe or has a right to judge, but also
to a considerable segment of his public, intellectual, social, and
moral existence. He must reach decisions among a multiplicity
of possible modes of subjective perception and personal reaction,
and no authority assumes responsibility in his stead for the soundness and the future effects of the decisions which are his alone.

What the "Crime" of Galileo
May Really Have Been Meant to Be

As the interpreter of his own works, Brecht endeavored to
convince us that the essence of man is sociality. Whoever plays
his role without banning his individuality from the stage, whoever
fails to identify himself with the superego of the authorities, does
not live up to the demands of his role and becomes a social criminal. Regardless of what the scope of Brecht's talents might have
been in their objective potentialities, subjectively he sacrificed
the full deployment of his human and artistic personality to a
system that relieved him of individual responsibility. Such was
the price he was ready to pay for a restraintless "privatistic" life,
though always with the implication that he could regard his re-
nunciation as a sacrifice for the benefit of mankind, that is to say,
for a goal of infinitely greater worth than the freedom of art and
science. Assuming that this was indeed the way Brecht understood
himself and his work, we recognize at last a credible way of rec-
onciling the multifarious interpretations which he himself ap-

plied to the treason of Galileo. Seen from this angle, the fact that
Brecht offered—successively and simultaneously—the most different interpretations of Galileo's "crime" (presenting it as a
betrayal of reason, a betrayal of science, a betrayal of mankind,
a betrayal of his profession), this fact can only signify that the
sole function of all his explanations was to conceal his real intent.
The true treason of Galileo, his "social criminality" that Brecht
proclaimed so emphatically, did not consist in his recantation but
in his persistence, despite his recantation, in indulging his scientific vice, that is to say, in refusing to obey the authorities with their
concern for the objective well-being of mankind.[57] It is this insubordination on the part of Galileo that Brecht could not forgive.
Galileo rebelled against the authority that at the time was responsible for mankind and—without regard to the social consequences of his actions—laid the foundation for the future
production of the atom bomb. It is the little monk who thus
appears to be the mouthpiece of Brecht himself and not the edi-
torializing Galileo of Scene 13. The authorities decide what truth
can be divulged and how much of it. During Galileo's lifetime
and in the country where he lived, this decision was for the Church
to reach; during Brecht's lifetime it was for the Central Committee of the German Communist Party and the Social Unity Party
to do so.

"From one day to the next, the biography of the founder of
modern physics read differently. The infernal effect of the great
bomb cast a new and sharper light on the conflict of Galileo with
the authorities of his age." [58] This reflection of Brecht's, quoted
from the preface to the American version of *The Life of Galileo*,
remains meaningless in any other perspective. The Church knew
better than Galileo what the outcome of his science was going to
be. When Brecht decided to go to East Berlin, he decided for
himself that obedience to a power embodying a higher historical
wisdom had priority over truth and truthfulness. The treason of
Galileo consisted in his disobedience to the Church whose authority he did recognize in principle. "It is important for the
stage directors to realize that this play is bound to lose a great
part of its effectiveness when its performance shows primarily a
tendency in opposition to the Catholic Church. . . . Modern science

is a legitimate daughter of the Church; it has achieved emancipation and has turned against its mother. In the play before us, the Church simply functions as the authority—even where it opposes freedom of investigation. Since science was a branch of theology, the Church, being the spiritual authority, represents the ultimate court of scientific appeal. . . ." [59] "In this play the Church represents primarily the authority; as types the Church dignitaries are to correspond to our officials and bankers." [60]

Sixteen years after the original composition of Brecht's *Life of Galileo* in Denmark and ten years after the restyling undertaken in the American version to fit the figure of Charles Laughton, Galileo Galilei finally reached the status of the only guilty one, of the criminal, of the scoundrel. It was he who was declared responsible for Hiroshima and for the corruption of bourgeois science in general. But the Church was absolved. It did what an authority must reasonably be expected to do in dealing with a renitent individualist who fails to understand the objective goals of the world spirit.

Brecht never openly opposed the communist system either during his Berlin years before 1933 or later in East Berlin. He did have disagreements, he did extricate himself trickily from many obligations, and he did—on occasion, for the benefit of a very small select circle—voice criticism (as, for instance, of Stalin whom he called "murderer of the people emeritus"), but he never resisted or contradicted, never, that is, in a way to attract the charge of being a revisionist. His contacts with the Harich group, for instance, were entirely noncommittal. They were of no benefit to the members of that group and involved no risks to himself. Among all the theoretical utterances of Brecht's on political matters, there is not one to suggest that he ever attempted to think through for himself the nature and the implications of Marxism. To Brecht, communism performed the functions of a doctrine of salvation to which the individual must submit and to which he can leave the entire responsibility for the well-being of mankind. It would otherwise be utterly incomprehensible that the critical reflections of his Marxist teachers Korsch and Sternberg never induced Brecht to derive any kind of inferences or conclusions of his own.

Galileo submitted to a superior force; Brecht voluntarily sought submission. Galileo was a stubborn individualist; Brecht strove to be a teacher's pet in the school of socialism. But as a rebel against the authorities, Galileo was not only the antipode of Brecht; he also was—as one who indulged his art in secret like a vice—an object of identification for Brecht. The increasingly emphasized characterization of Galileo as a voluptuous cynic who destroys the life of his daughter becomes comprehensible only when it is taken to be—unconsciously-consciously—a self-portrait of the author.[61] Brecht himself saw that he was a voluptuous cynic whose social conformism concealed his private anarchy, an individual concerned about his very personal well-being who utilized the entire pompous apparatus of political and aesthetic ideals for no purpose other than that of protecting his concept of life and of assuring its implementation. "If Galileo had known how to maintain himself in the good graces of the Fathers and of the College, he would be living in the world as one crowned with fame, and none of all these adversities would have befallen him. He would have been at liberty to write at will on anything and everything, even on the movement of the earth." [62] These golden words of wisdom which Father Grienberger offered to Galileo after his condemnation as a belated advice—which Galileo had failed and continued to fail to heed—extol a rule of conduct that Brecht observed unswervingly throughout his life.

III
Exhibits

The Life of the Historical Galileo Galilei

Galileo Galilei was born in Pisa on February 15, 1564, three days before the death of Michelangelo. His father, Vincenzio Galilei, was a Florentine nobleman, his mother came from the Ammanati family of Pescia. Vincenzio had made a name for himself by his writings on the theory of music, in particular on the relationship of music to mathematics. There is reason to believe that—like many respectable citizens of Florence—he earned his living in the cloth trade.

It thus appears that Galileo's father already was a man of culture with an open mind for the arts and the sciences. It also appears that Vincenzio already was a man disinclined to trust arguments not arising from his own experience. In the *Dialogue on Old and New Music*, published in 1581, he wrote, for instance: "It is my opinion that the censure of unreason is deserved by those who strive to prove the validity of a statement by relying exclusively on the weight of the authorities without making use of any other argument. I for one desire that controversial questions be posed freely and be debated freely as behooves any man honestly questing after the truth."

Vincenzio Galilei was not wealthy, but he managed to give his son Galileo a commensurate education. The boy grew up into a promising young man. He manifested considerable talent for drawing, was a master on the lute, and took an intense interest in the classical works of Italian literature. From these early days we have essays written by Galileo on Dante, Ariosto, and Tasso, and also an unfinished play.

On September 5, 1580, Galileo Galilei's name was inscribed on the rolls of the University of Pisa. In compliance with the wishes of his father, who hoped for a remunerative career for his son, Galileo began to study medicine. This he continued for three years until the influence of a friend of the family led him to concern himself with mathematics. This science cast such a spell on him that he decided, initially against the resistance of his father, to give up medicine in order to devote himself exclusively to the study of mathematics and physics. In those days the mathematical sciences were not as yet particularly respected, and it is quite understandable that the father objected to his son's decision to follow a career of so little promise.

During Galileo's fourth year at the university his father applied for a stipend for him. This application was turned down, and in 1585 Galileo was back in Florence where he continued his mathematical studies without so far having taken any examination. Throughout the following four years Galileo was obliged, for financial reasons, to make his living as a private tutor, but he did manage, at that early time, to compose a number of minor essays on mathematical subjects and to establish far-flung connections with influential personalities. Finally, in the summer of 1589, he was appointed Professor of Mathematics at the University of Pisa. His yearly emolument amounted to sixty scudi. (In the same year the occupant of the chair for medicine at the University of Pisa drew 2000 scudi.) For many years to come, Galileo was hence obliged to eke out his living by giving private lessons.

Under these conditions he was on the lookout for a possibility of moving to some other university, and in 1592 the efforts of his most influential patrons, the Marchese and the Cardinal del Monte, were successful in procuring for him a call to take over the chair for mathematics at the University of Padua which belonged at the time to the Republic of Venice. Here at Padua Galileo taught and worked for eighteen years until in 1610 he was called to the University of Florence. During his Padua years he carried out his pioneering investigations and made his pioneering discoveries regarding the laws of gravity, of inertia, of the movement of the pendulum, and of consonance and resonance. From this period we have from him the statement which characterizes his overall approach to scientific probing: "The man who undertakes to solve a scientific question without the help of mathematics undertakes the impossible. We must measure what is mensurable and make mensurable what cannot be measured." Galileo developed the experimental method. He constructed various machines for the Republic of Venice. He invented the proportional compass and an early form of the thermoscope which is to be regarded as a precursor of the thermometer.

Among the earliest proofs of his acceptance of the Copernican theory is a letter going back to August 4, 1597, addressed to
the then most famous German astronomer, Johannes Kepler, in
which Galileo acknowledged having received a copy of Kepler's
work, *Mysterium Cosmographicum*. Galileo did not, however,
admit in any public statement that he was a Copernican. The
letter to Kepler contains the following passage: "I shall read your
work in full confidence of the outcome and am convinced that I
shall find in it much that is excellent. I shall do so the more
eagerly since for years I have been an adherent to the Copernican
view which explains to me the causes of many natural phenomena
that remain utterly inexplicable within the limits of the commonly accepted hypothesis. To disprove this latter I have compiled numerous arguments but I dare not bring them to the light
of public attention for fear lest my fate become that of our master
Copernicus who, although in the esteem of some his fame has
come to be immortal, stands in the opinion of infinitely many
(for such are the numbers of fools) as an object of ridicule and
derision. Surely, I would not hesitate to publish my speculations
if there were more men of the kind of which you are one. Since
such is not the case I shall bide my time."

To appreciate fully this reserve we must bear in mind that
Giordano Bruno, whose career was to end in 1600 at the stake,
had been a prisoner at the Castle of Sant' Angelo ever since 1593,
when he had been condemned as a heretic because he had drawn
inferences from the Copernican cosmological system that ran
strictly counter to the cosmic order reflected in Scripture. The
scientists of the time were unquestioning followers of Aristotle
and Ptolemy, and the doctrine of Copernicus was regarded as an
utterly fantastic hypothesis, so that Galileo was indeed justified
in his fear that a public profession of Copernicanism on his part
would undermine his reputation as a scientist. A point to be emphasized in this connection is that all the extant writings of Galileo make abundantly clear that he was never prepared to interpret
the Copernican principles—as Giordano Bruno had done—in a
sense running counter to the tenets of the Christian faith. On the
contrary, to the end of his life Galileo remained convinced that
the doctrine of the sun's being the center of the universe with the

earth revolving around it could very well be reconciled with the teachings of the Bible, provided we are able and willing to read the Bible correctly. In any event, there is no document to suggest that Galileo's scientific convictions were ever the cause of a serious crisis in the continuity of his religious faith. As we read his works and the testimonials of his contemporaries relative to his works and to his person we cannot but conclude—provided we are still able to read without prejudice—that Galileo was not only the man whose appearance marked the beginnings of the age of science but also the first representative of the breed of naturalists who see nothing difficult in the reconciliation of their faith in eschatological truths with their keen sense for the natural truths in the world of realities.

We must further consider that initially the Church itself saw no reason to condemn the Copernican theory. It is true, Copernicus hesitated almost to the end of his life to publish his work, *De Revolutionibus orbium coelestium*, but when he finally did release it for publication, he dedicated it to Pope Paul III, being fully convinced that his concept of the structural coherence of the cosmos would make the mircale of Creation still more miraculous that it appeared to be in the Ptolemaic interpretation.

A decisive turn in Galileo's career as a scientist—and also in the gradual coming to a head of his subsurface conflict with the Church—was brought about by the invention of the telescope. The priority for this invention must be conceded to Dutch lens grinders who applied in 1608 to the States General for a letter patent. It is likely that the earliest rumor of the invention of a telescope reached Italy by way of France. There is also some evidence in support of the assumption that as early as 1609 samples of actual telescopes arrived for the first time in Italy. We do not know when and through whom Galileo learned about the Dutch invention. What is known as a fully documented fact is that as soon as the news reached him of the successful mounting of glasses in a way that made it possible to make distant objects appear near, Galileo forthwith set to work to build such an instrument himself. It seems that his efforts were crowned with success in August 1609. He immediately presented his construction to the City Council of Venice and claimed, in doing to, that he was the inventor of the

telescope. On August 21, 1609, he demonstrated from the belfry of
Saint Mark's the astounding capabilities of his instrument to the
procurator Antonio Priuli and seven other Venetian patricians.
Three days later he presented the telescope as a gift to the Signoria
of Venice, writing in the accompanying letter among other things:
"The advantages are inestimable that can accure to all ventures
on land and on the sea from the possibility provided by this instrument of seeing objects closer by. On the sea we shall be able
to discover the vessels and the sails of the enemy two hours before
we ourselves are within the enemy's sight. As in this fashion we
can distinguish the numbers and types of the enemy's ships we
can evaluate his strength and reach a decision as to whether we
should take up the chase, accept battle, or withdraw. In the same
way we are able on land to have the enemy's camp or his fortifica-
tions inside his strongholds observed from high places and can
also see in the open field to our own advantage at his movements
and preparations and distinguish them in great detail."

The very next day, on August 25, the City Council of Venice
decided to grant Galileo, in recognition of his services to the republic, lifetime tenure in his professorship at Padua and to increase his yearly emolument to 1000 florins.

The insinuation that Galileo practiced deceit in order to secure for himself such advantages became so outspoken that Galileo felt it necessary, half a year after the presentation of the
telescope, to use the opportunity of the publication of his *Sidereus
Nuncius* to explain in detail his share in the invention: "Some
ten months ago," he wrote, "the rumor reached me that a Belgian
had put together a perspicillum by means of which objects, though
far removed from the observer, could be distinctly seen as though
nearby, and of this marvelous effect a number of illustrations was
reported to which some lent credence while others did not. Several days later letters from the eminent Frenchman Jacques Bado-
vere of Paris provided me with confirmation of the rumor. That
was the event that decided me to bend all my thinking upon the
elucidation of the causes and the discovery of the means that
might lead to the invention of a similar instrument, and this I
accomplished successfully a short while thereafter, using as my
basis the principles of the refraction of light. First I made a tube

of lead at the end of which I mounted two glass lenses, both plain on one side but one spherically convex and the second concave on the other side. When I then brought my eye close to the concave glass I saw the objects markedly enlarged and nearer, for they appeared three times closer and nine times larger than they were seen with the naked eye."

In judging the deceptive maneuver of which Galileo had doubtless made himself guilty, we need to consider that in his age nothing existed that could be compared to our patent laws and also that the Galilean construction exceeded in its effectiveness the already existing telescopes by a very wide margin. Galileo could thus very well lay claim to the fame of having been the first to construct a "perspicillum" that was of use for the purposes of astronomical observations.

The most important discoveries which Galileo was enabled to make by means of his telescope were accomplished by him in short order. During the interval from January 7 to 13, 1610, he saw through the telescope "the moons of Jupiter." This represented the first empirical proof of the Copernican thesis that there are celestial bodies revolving in regular orbits around another while all of them together revolve in a larger circle around the center of the planetary system. In other words, there was now proof of the existence of celestial bodies that, as Copernicus had taught, do not revolve around the earth but around some other planet.

In Rome, too, the new discoveries were by no means greeted with indifference. To be sure, the Jesuit Christopher Clavius, the most renowned mathematician of the Collegium Romanum had remarked in response to the first news of the discovery of the moons of Jupiter that "all that was necessary was to produce a glass with the property of generating stars which could then be observed through it." But on December 17, 1610, after he had had an opportunity to verify Galileo's observations by means of a telescope, he wrote to Galileo as follows: "You must have wondered why I did not reply sooner to your letter of September 17. The reason is that I expected from day to day that you would come to Rome and also that I first wanted to try to see the Medicean planets myself. I can now report that we did see them here

in Rome on repeated occasions in most perfect distinctness. At
the end of this letter I shall note down several observations that
demonstrate most clearly that they are not fixed stars but planets,
that is, wandering stars, for they change their positions with respect to one another and with respect to Jupiter. You are indeed
deserving of great praise for having been the first to observe these
things. Even before that, we had been able to distinguish a great
number of stars in the Pleiades, the Crab, Orion, and the Milky
Way that cannot be seen without an instrument. As for the moon,
I was surprised to see how uneven and rough it is when it is not
full. Truly, this instrument would be invaluable if handling it
were not so cumbersome."

During the time of these discoveries and discussions Galileo
was also preoccupied with the preparations for his removal to
Florence. As early as October 1609 Galileo had been to Florence
at the personal request of Grand Duke Cosimo II who wished to
be shown the telescope by its maker. At that early time, only two
months after the Republic of Venice had officially honored him,
he was quite outspoken at the court of Florence in regard to his
wish to return home and to enter into the service of the prince
of whose personal benevolence he felt assured. Galileo had been
one of Cosimo's tutors, and in February 1609, on the occasion of
Cosimo's succession to the throne, he had made the following
statement in response to the intimation that specific wishes he
might feel inclined to express would be lent a receptive ear: "I
have now spent some twenty years—the best of my life—investing
(as one might say) in the retail trade, at any first-comer's request,
the modest talents that God granted me and that fell to my share
as a result of my efforts in my profession. If therefore the Grand
Duke, through the goodness of his heart and the ability of his
thought, were willing to grant me what I might wish, apart from
the pleasure of being allowed to serve him, I confess that my
thoughts would be preoccupied with the objective of gaining sufficient leisure and peace of mind to enable me to complete, before
the end of my life, three great works on which I am now at work,
in order to publish them with some fame accruing to me and to
him who would have furthered my endeavors in these fields, and
possibly, for the adepts of science, with greater, more universal,

and more lasting benefits than could flow from what I would otherwise be able to accomplish in the years that are still left to me. . . . I do not believe I can find greater leisure than is now my share in any place where I would not be freed from the necessity of providing for my house and my family by public lectures and private tutoring. Furthermore, for reasons too involved to explain briefly, I would not like to carry on this kind of activity in any other city. Yet, the freedom which I have been enjoying is not enough, for I am obliged to sacrifice at the request of one individual or another many hours of the day and often enough the very best. It runs counter to custom to accept a salary from a republic, however brilliant and high-minded it may be, without serving the public, for a man who wants to derive profit from the public must give the public its due, which is quite different from satisfying the wishes of one individual. As long as I am able to lecture and to perform my duties, no one in a republic can relieve me of such obligations and still allow me to draw my income. In short, the condition I wish for I cannot hope to be granted by anyone but an absolute monarch. . . . Yet, Sire, I would be loath to have you derive from what I said the impression that my demands are unreasonable and that I desire an emolument without merit and without performing services, for such is not my thought. As for the merit, I have in my possession various inventions, each one of which, placed at the disposal of a great prince who takes an interest in it, may well be enough to satisfy my needs throughout the remaining years of my life, for experience tells me that things of possibly much lesser worth often entail great advantages for their inventors. And it has always been my thought to offer my findings to my native lord and master so that it be within his decision to dispose at will of them and their author and to take—if he so pleases—not only the ore but also the mine, for everyday I make new findings and would find still more if I had more leisure and if I had more helpers at my disposal on whom I could call for the various required experiments. . . . As for the day-to-day service, there is only one mode I loathe, the meretricious obligation to place myself and my efforts at the disposal of anyone willing to pay the price. To serve a prince or a great lord and those near him will not be hardship to me but a thing I shall desire and cherish. . . . Since you, Sire, touch upon the question of my present revenues, I may report that my official salary has been 520 florins and that I can expect it with certainty to be increased to the same number of scudi within a few months, at the time of the renewal of my employment. This amount I can add to considerably, for I derive for the needs of the household a substantial contribution from boarding students and from the remuneration for private lectures. This latter amount is as large as I wish to make it. I say this since I tend to avoid rather than to seek opportunities to present many lectures, free time being infinitely more what I desire than gold, for I know that it will be much harder for me to acquire wealth sufficient to assure me renown before the world than to carry out investigations to assure me a modicum of fame."

In the spring of 1610 he pressed for a decision emphasizing once again his hope that in Florence he be given the opportunity to continue and complete his scientific works without the need, which he faced in Padua, to worry about lectures. He requested that he be given the title of Philosopher to the Grand Duke. The letter in which he made these points indicates that Galileo was ready to accept any kind of financial arrangement as long as he was given the position which alone, in his opinion, would afford him the freedom of continuing his scientific work. The court at Florence acceded to his wishes, and on July 10, 1610, Galileo received the appointment as "Mathematicus Primarius and Philosophus to the Grand Duke" and "Mathematicus Primarius of the University of Pisa." Two months later, on September 12, 1610, he arrived in Florence.

It has been surmised that Galileo's decision to leave Padua was in part determined by factors involving his home life. Since 1599, Galileo had been living in an extramarital relationship with the Venetian woman Maria Gamba. It appears that Galileo's mother and Maria Gamba were utterly uncongenial, and the desire to escape the resulting annoyances may indeed have played a role in Galileo's wish to leave Padua. From his relations with Maria Gamba, which ended with the removal of the Galilei family to Florence, Galileo had three children. His oldest daughter, Virginia, had gone ahead to Florence with Galileo's mother. The younger daughter, Livia, was taken to Florence by Galileo himself in September, while his four-year-old son, Vincenzio, stayed with his mother for a few years until the latter married a resident of Padua.

Galileo's sudden removal to Florence aroused great displeasure both in Padua and Venice. It seemed hard to understand how he could have preferred a position at the court of a prince to the position to which he had just been appointed in the service of the Republic of Venice, and there was also the point, hard to excuse and impossible to forgive, that he deserted his friends and patrons in Padua without, apparently, having served notice that he wished to give up his chair at the university. The concern which was felt for his future career is reflected in a letter addressed to Galileo by Giovanni Francesco Sagredo, a Venetian diplomat and very close friend of Galileo's, when he, Sagredo, returned from a mission in 1611 to find that Galileo had left.

"You now are," Sagredo wrote, "in your most noble homeland, but it is also true that you have left a place where your well-being seemed assured. You are now in the service of your native prince, who is great and excelling, a youth of whom the best may be expected, but here you were in a position to give orders to those who order others of whom they are the rulers, and you were bound in duty to serve no one but yourself, as though you were the ruler of the world. . . . The excellent character and the nobility of your prince justify the hope that your devotion and your deserts will be respected and rewarded, but who can be certain on the stormy waters of life at court that he will not, in the raging winds of jealousy, meet with, let us not say disaster, but trouble and unrest? I do not wish to take into consideration that as the prince advances in years, his temperament and his inclinations as well as his interest must needs undergo a change, for I am told that his qualities are so firmly rooted that ever more abundant and ever better fruit may be expected to be borne by them; but who can foretell what the effect may be of those countless and incalculable vicissitudes of worldly existence if they are aggravated by the deceit of evil minds in envious men who may strive by slanderous means to arouse and nurture false conceptions in the mind of the prince, exploiting precisely his justice and nobility in their endeavor to ruin a good man? . . . A prince will take delight for a while in what to him are entertaining curiosities, but as soon as greater things claim his interest, he is apt to turn elsewhere. Surely, I do not doubt that the Grand Duke will derive pleasure from surveying, through your perspicillum, the city of Florence and other places in the vicinity, but when his purposes demand that he should observe what events are taking place throughout all of Italy, in France, in Spain, in Germany, and in the Near East, he will put aside your glass. And even if we assume that your inventive genius succeeds in constructing another instrument fit to satisfy that vaster requirement, who can imagine a glass that permits its user to distinguish the wise from the fools, good advice from bad, an understanding architect from the opinionated and ignorant builder? Who does not know that the decision in these matters is reached by a court of justice made up of an infinite number of infinite fools whose votes are counted but not weighed? And finally," the letter closes, "there is the fact, which gives me great concern, that you find yourself in a place where, we are told, the fathers of the Society of Jesus enjoy great repute."

That Galileo should have failed to take into consideration the last fact cited by Sagredo is proof of his naive innocence. He left the free soil of the Republic of Venice to accept the patronship of a prince who personally was well disposed toward him but who nonetheless depended on Rome, implying that Galileo was henceforth at the mercy of the Inquisition. In Padua, on Venetian soil, this would not have been the case. As recently as 1606, when the Pope had laid the Republic of Venice under the great interdict because of its lack of compliancy, it had been possible for the Republic to respond by banning the Jesuits forever from its territories.

Meanwhile the debate on the astronomical discoveries of Galileo and their implications continued. Galileo had been cautious enough to avoid in his publication, *Sidereus Nuncius* (1610), any reference to a direct link between his discoveries and the Copernican system. He had strictly limited himself to presenting the facts as he had found them to be. Still, there was violent opposition on the part of many scientists and philosophers who sensed that the Aristotelian-Ptolemaic world as the ultimate foundation of all their concepts was being threatened.

To what extent this resistance embittered Galileo is evidenced by a letter he addressed to Kepler under date of August 19, 1610. "You are the first and virtually the only one," he wrote, "to give my findings full credence, for you are able to think independently and possess the powers of a lofty mind. . . . In Pisa, Florence, Bologna, Venice, and Padua, many have seen the [Medicean] planets, but none speaks up and all are wavering, for most of them recognize neither Jupiter nor Mars and hardly the moon as planets. What shall we do? Shall we conduct ourselves after the model of Democritus or of Heraclitus? I deem it wise, my dear Kepler, that we merely laugh about the stupidity of the crowd. What do you think of the first philosophers here at the university whom I assured a thousand times that I was ready to submit my work to them of my own free will but who display the stubbornness of a snake that has eaten its fill and want to see neither planets nor moon nor telescope? This tribe believes that philosophy is a book, somewhat like the Aeneid or the Odyssey, and that truth need not be looked for in the cosmos but (and I quote) in a comparison of the texts."

It appears that Galileo understood clearly that the continuation of his work was inseparably linked to the recognition of the Copernican doctrine and that the decision as to the recognition of this doctrine could be reached only in Rome. It was, therefore, his endeavor to find an opportunity to report in Rome on his discoveries and to discuss them there with the mathematicians and astronomers at the Vatican. In January 1611 he addressed a petition for an affidavit to the Florentine minister Vinta, including in it the following statement: "The new facts that have been brought to light through my observations imply with respect to the doctrine of celestial movements the necessity of extensions and changes of such importance that under their influence this science must needs appear as largely new and, as it were, as transferred from night to day."

In March 1611, Galileo—equipped with several good telescopes—arrived in Rome. His stay there took on the appearance of a triumph. The experts' opinion, which Cardinal Bellarmin requested from the mathematicians of the Collegium Romanum on the new celestial observations, confirmed the discoveries described by Galileo. In other words, the Jesuits pronounced openly in Galileo's favor, and Pope Paul V, too, received Galileo and assured him of his personal good will. The great success of Galileo's trip to Rome is reflected in the letter that Cardinal del Monte addressed to Grand Duke Cosimo on May 31, 1611.: "His discoveries have been recognized by all deserving and knowledgeable men in this city not only as true and real but also as full of wonders. If this were still the Roman Republic of old, surely a statue of him would be erected on the Capitol to honor his worth as is due."

Yet, at about the same time, on May 6, 1611, the Roman clergyman Paolo Gualdo, a friend of Galileo's, expressed grave concern. In a letter addressed by him to Galileo we find the following passage: "So far I have found no philosopher and no astronomer ready to agree with your contention that the earth moves, and still less would the theologians be inclined to agree. Reflect, therefore, and think twice before you come out in public with this view of yours in the form of a definite assertion, for there is much that can be said in a private debate that cannot be maintained as true before the world, especially if one faces the opposition of concepts accepted by everyone, one may say, since the time of Creation. Forgive me, but what makes me speak in this manner is the great concern I have for your reputation. It seems to me that you have acquired your full share of fame through your observations in the moon, the four planets, and the like, without having to enter the lists in defense of a viewpoint which runs so much counter to the insight and the powers of comprehension of men because there are only a very few who understand ought of the observation of celestial signs and aspects."

From the minutes of a meeting of the General Congregation of the Inquisition of May 17, it appears that the publicly averred assent to Galileo's discoveries was a façade concealing an attitude of marked criticism toward him. The document contains this note: "The proceedings in the case of Doctor Cesare Cremonini are to be examined to determine whether the professor of philosophy and mathematics, Galileo, is mentioned in them." Cremonini was Philosophus Primarius at the University of Padua and had aroused the displeasure of the Jesuits by taking a determined stand against their activities at the university. In addition, there were rumors imputing atheistic ideas to him.

The real reason for the distrust of the Jesuits was most probably the fact that in the spring of 1611, when during his stay at Rome Galileo had several conversations with Cardinal Bellarmin, he appears to have left the Cardinal with the distinct impression that despite the restraint he imposed upon himself for the present, he cherished the hope that he might in the long run induce the Church to recognize the Copernican theory.

In any event, throughout the ensuing years Galileo found himself again confronted with the hostile opposition of the Aristotelians. His investigations of the laws governing the behavior of swimming bodies made it necessary for him for the first time to oppose openly a thesis of Aristotelian physics. His preoccupation with the sunspots drew him into further violent debates and won him in particular the embittered enmity of the Jesuit Christoph Scheiner who not only doubted Galileo's interpretation but also claimed priority in the scientific study of the phenomenon of the sunspots.

In April 1613 Galileo published his monograph on the sunspots, consisting of three letters written by him in the course of the two preceding years to the Augsburg councilman Marcus Welser and containing unmistakably Copernican ideas. The crucial thesis in this monograph is the supposition that the sun itself revolves around its axis and that the direction in which it does so coincides with that of the movements of the planets.

The third letter to Welser, dated December 1, 1612, closes with the following words: "Whether the events will occur in precisely the way I predict or in some other way, one thing is certain, this star [that is Saturn] and possibly to no less an extent the phenomenon of the sickle shape of Venus contribute marvelously to the harmony of the great Copernican system of which the complete revelation is propelled by so favorable a wind, with so shining a light showing us the way, that there is little left for us to fear of darkness or hostile countercurrents."

The letters on the sunspots prove that Galileo remained determined to win recognition for the Copernican view of the movement of the earth and that it was simultaneously his hope that he
would be able to convince Rome that such a recognition would
not only be advantageous to scientific truth but might in the long
run be in the interest of the Church itself. His opponents, however, took his monograph on the sunspots as their cue to charge
him publicly with the crime of heresy.

In the entourage of the Grand Duke the question was likewise
the topic of heated debates. In them Galileo's position was defended by Father Castelli from the very beginning of his appointment as Professor of Mathematics at Pisa (which he had received
in November 1613 on the basis of a recommendation by Galileo).
Castelli reported to Galileo in writing on his relevant conversations at court, and Galileo replied in a detailed communication
toward the end of December 1613. Here he concerned himself in
particular with the question as to how the doctrine of the movement of the earth could be reconciled with the statements in Holy
Scripture. "Since, then," Galileo wrote, "Holy Scripture not only
permits but in fact demands in many passages an interpretation
diverging from what the words as such appear to say, I opine that
Holy Scripture must be made to rank last as an authority in
mathematical discussions. . . . It seems to me, therefore, that no
work of nature that is taught us by our eyes' experience or that
is otherwise demonstrable by proof should be cast into doubt by
reason of passages in Holy Scripture which contains words by the
thousands that admit of diverse interpretations, for no statement
in Holy Scripture is subject to laws as rigid as those governing
every work of nature." And further along: "Since it is patently
impossible for two truths to be at odds, it is the task of the wise
exegetes of Holy Scripture to endeavor to find the true meaning
of the statements to establish their accord with those necessary
inferences which must be made by reason of definite evidence
or certain proof." And again: "I am inclined to believe that it is
the function of the authority of Holy Scripture to convince men
of those truths which are necessary for the salvation of their souls
and which—since they exceed all human understanding—cannot
acquire credibility by any science other than that of the revelation

of the Holy Ghost. That the very God who gave us senses, reason, and judgment should forbid us their use, that He should insist on providing us with those insights by other means, though we are able to obtain them ourselves by virtue of the qualifications just mentioned, that—methinks—is a thing I am not obligated to believe. This applies in particular to those sciences of which Holy Scripture contains only minor fragments with diverse inferences, which is precisely the case of astronomy, for astronomy plays so unimportant a role in Holy Scripture that not even all the planets are as much as mentioned."

Neither Castelli nor Galileo was minded to treat this letter as a confidential communication. Castelli had it make the rounds in Florence, and within a short period of time a whole series of copies were made of it. It is not surprising, therefore, that the letter soon fell into the hands of Galileo's adversaries. Among these, two Dominican monks, the Fathers Caccini and Lorini, were particularly articulate. Caccini attacked Galileo publicly from the pulpit on the fourth Sunday of Advent of the year 1614, and on February 7, 1615, a copy of the letter was sent to the Cardinal Secretary of the Roman Inquisition. The covering note, composed by Father Lorini, contains this sentence: "Aware that beyond the obligations shared by every good Christian, all brothers of Saint Dominicus, though particularly the theologians and preachers among them, bear the never ending duty imposed upon them by their Holy Father to be the white and black dogs of the Congregation of the Holy Office, I, who am the least among all and who am dedicated to you, my most illustrious lord, in unqualified obedience, have decided—since a document has come to my attention which is going from hand to hand in these parts, originating among those who call themselves Galileans and who maintain that the earth moves while the heavens stand firm in accordance with the teachings of Copernicus and since in this document, according to the judgment of all of us fathers of this God-fearing monastery of Saint Mark, many statements are contained which appear to us either suspect or temerarious, since, despite these facts, I see that the document circulates without being intercepted by any of the superiors, although those responsible for the document aim to interpret Holy Scripture in their own way and against the accepted interpretation of the Holy Fathers, upholding an opinion entirely and evidently contrary to Holy Scripture, and since I have been told that these men speak with little respect of the Holy Fathers of old and of Saint Thomas, trampling under foot the entire philosophy of Aristotle of which scholastic theology makes so much use and, all in all, uttering a thousand impertinences in order to prove the enlightenment of their wits and spreading them throughout the entire city which, thanks to the wholesome disposition of its inhabitants and thanks, also, to the vigilance of our most illustrious princes, has remained firm in its catholicity—for all these reasons, then, I have decided to send you, my most illustrious lord, this document so that you—who are filled with a holy zeal and are qualified, through your high position and together with your most illustrious colleagues, to keep watch in such matters—may be in a position, if it appears to you that the document requires correction, to apply the means you deem necessary so that the error, initially small, may not become great in the outcome."

The denunciation of Galileo was on the agenda of a session of the Inquisition as early as February 25. On March 20, 1615, Caccini was questioned by the Commissioner General of the Inquisition and stated into the record that it was an open secret in Florence that Galileo advocated the Copernican view of the movement of the earth. He did concede that he had never met the man in person and that, though some regarded him as "suspect in matters of faith," others judged him to be "a good Catholic." In the course of the hearing with Caccini on the witness stand, so many suspicious details were recorded that the Pope ordered the Inquisitor at Florence to summon and interrogate additional witnesses.

Initially Galileo himself, as well as his friends in Florence and Rome, were quite unaware of the proceedings that had been set in motion against him. In fact, his contacts in Rome—the Cardinals del Monte and Bellarmin—kept assuring him that he had nothing to fear so long as he did not trespass the confines of physics and mathematics and abstained from all interpretations of Holy Scripture. His friend, Prince Cesi, who was constantly in touch with the Vatican, was even more confident. He thought that the time was not far off when anyone could freely present the Copernican thesis "just like any other physical or mathematical topic."

Toward the end of 1615, however, Galileo realized that an intrigue against him was afoot in Rome. His main concern was to prevent a condemnation of the Copernican doctrine, and he decided, confident of his good connections, to go to Rome himself. Cosimo provided him with letters of recommendation to a number of cardinals. The letter to Cardinal del Monte contains the following passage: "I gladly acceded to his request, for I have always regarded him as a man who, righteous in attitude, respects honor and conscience, and because I am convinced, for that very reason, that he will, when allowed to appear and to speak in person, be able to clear himself sufficiently and to ward off with ease the attacks directed against him. In this respect, I believe, he is not in need of my protection. In any event, I would never extend my protection to anyone whose endeavor it is to use my good will to cover a violation, particularly in matters of religion and of the morality of his conduct. There is only one reason that I wish him to have in his possession this letter to you, illustrious Lord, to wit, that you man hear him with due friendliness as one of my servants whom I esteem and that you grant him your favors as he deserves them, seeing to it, in particular, that he will be questioned by men of insight and fairness of spirit who refuse to lend an ear to impassioned and ill-willed persecutions."

On this occasion, not less than before, Galileo was received in Rome with all the respect due him, and there was no official examination by the Inquisition. There can, however, be no doubt but that he was led in conversation to speak about the subject matter that had given rise to the accusations against him. The records show—and this conclusion is borne out by the subsequent line of action of the Inquisition—that there was a prevailing desire to spare Galileo and that the major concern in those years was not to keep Galileo at bay but to stem the tide of what was regarded as the ever-growing danger of the spread of the Copernican doctrine.

That Galileo gauged the situation correctly is apparent from a lengthy essay that he completed in 1615 under the guise of a

letter addressed to the Dowager Grandduchess of Tuscany but
which was not published in printed form at the time. There is no
reason to regard the arguments in this work as a tactical maneuver. We must rather accept the premise that Galileo presented
here his relationship to the Church and to the Christian faith as
what he himself felt it to be. "I honor and respect," he wrote,
"Holy Scripture, the sainted theologians, and the counsels of the
Church as the highest authority and would regard it as temerarious in the extreme to undertake to contradict them insofar as
they are invoked in keeping with the prescriptions of the Holy
Church. But I also believe that it is not erroneous to speak up
when there is a possibility of assuming that they are invoked in
the personal interest of the speakers who wish to exploit them in
a way not in harmony with the objectives of the Holy Church. . . .
To order the teachers of astronomy that they themselves should
take charge of protecting themselves against their own observations and proofs because those observations and proofs are bound
to be illusory, is bound to be sophistry, is to order them to do the
impossible, for the implication is that they are ordered not to
see what they see and not to understand what they understand
but to find in their search the opposite of what they hold in their
hands. To this end it would first be necessary to teach them how
to proceed in order that among the forces of the soul the one may
be in command over the other, the lower over the higher, so that
imagination and will become able and willing to believe the opposite of what reason comprehends. . . . If, in order to eradicate
this view and these teachings, it were enough to seal one individual's mouth (as possibly those try to convince themselves who
measure the judgment of others by their own and hence cannot
conceive that such a view will persist and attract advocates), it
would be extraordinarily easy to settle the matter. But that is
not the way things are. To implement such a decision, it would
not only be necessary to suppress the book of Copernicus and the
writings of the other authors adhering to the same doctrine, it
would also be necessary to forbid the entire science of astronomy
and, still more, to forbid men to look at the sky lest they see Mars
and Venus changing with their changing distance from the earth
to an apparent size that at certain times is forty and sixty times

larger than it is at others and lest that same Venus appear to them
now round and now sickle-shaped with delicately outlined horns
as well as many other things which the senses perceive and which
are in no way compatible with the Ptolemaic system while representing the strongest arguments for the Copernican. . . . To forbid
Copernicus now—when many new observations and the preoccupation of numerous scholars with the Copernican work make his
conclusions appear truer from day to day, revealing ever more
clearly how firmly his doctrine is rooted—although he was tolerated for many years while he had fewer advocates and seemed
less well confirmed, that, it seems to me, is as though one wanted
to oppose truth the more, wanted to conceal and repress truth
the more, the more evidently and clearly it comes to light. . . .
And if, without suppressing the book itself completely, the objective were only to condemn this specific view as erroneous, the
result, if I am not mistaken, would be a still greater damage to
the souls of men, for they would be in possession of the means to
prove a truth in which they are not allowed to believe without
committing a sin. . . . What else would that be than to act counter
to a hundred passages of Holy Scripture that teach us how the
glory and grandeur of the All-Highest is wonderfully apparent in
all His works and can be read in a divine way in the open books
of the heavens? Let no one assume that the sublime arts inscribed
in the pages of those books have been fully fathomed if one but
contemplates the brilliance of the sun and the stars and their rise
and descent. No, they contain secrets so deep and thoughts so
lofty that the wakeful nights, the toils and labors and studies of
hundreds of the keenest minds in thousands of years of unin-
terupted search have not sufficed to gauge them. In writing down
these reflections, which may seem remote from the field of my
calling, I am prompted by no motive other than that of my hope
that, by the side of the errors that may here appear, a few things
will be found of a kind apt and able to prompt others to derive
profit from them in the interest of the Holy Church when a decision is reached with regard to the Copernican doctrine and that
my reflections be accepted or utilized to the extent our superiors
may deem wise, it being my firm belief that in case the afore-stated
hope should prove to be vain it were best that these sheets be torn

into pieces and be cast into the fire, for I do not expect nor contemplate that through them I may reap a crop lacking in piety and failing to be in accord with the Catholic faith."

It was Galileo's passionate wish to do everything in his power to prevent a condemnation of the Copernican doctrine that induced him to stay on in Rome even after he had gained the impression that the proceedings against his person had been suspended. How he saw the problem at that time is apparent from two letters written by him on January 23 and February 16, 1616. The earlier of the two contains this passage: "External circumstances serve to increase the difficulties and the time requirements of the negotiations beyond the limits congruent with their nature, especially since I cannot speak freely to those with whom I am dealing lest I might harm one or another of my friends, just as those with whom I am dealing cannot speak freely to me lest they run the risk of making themselves liable to being most severely punished. It follows that I must proceed in my endeavors with great care and foresight, seeking out third persons who are qualified—albeit without cognizance of my purposes—to serve as my mediators in relation to the principals and who can arrange things so that, with the appearance of a coincidence but in fact at their request, I am admitted and thus in a position to bring up the matters that brought me here and to explain their implications in detail. Then, too, I must discuss specific points in writing and make sure that what I have written is passed on in secret to the right hands, for in many places it appears to be easier to arouse attention by means of a dead piece of paper than by means of the living voice, which is doubtless so because a man can concede, contradict, and weigh the arguments without having to blush when he peruses a manuscript with no witness other than himself in a position to observe his thinking. This will not occur quite so readily when what might make us change our minds lies open, as it were, to the eyes of the world. To carry on all these things in Rome, as a stranger, requires much effort and time, but the confident hope that I shall be able to bring to a successful conclusion the project in which I am engaged and the knowledge that it is a project of the greatest importance enable me to endure all the hardship with patience."

In the second letter, dated February 16, 1616, Galileo wrote: "The matter that brought me here has fully been taken care of as far as that part of it is concerned which affects my own person. That this is so I have been made to understand without qualifications and in the kindliest of ways by all the men in high places who have to do with these matters. The decision, they assure me, that has been reached reflects the clearest recognition not only of my blameless probity but also of the devilish malice and the devious intentions of my persecutors." And he added: "As far as this point is concerned, it is thus apparent that I could return home whenever I choose to. But my case is linked to a matter that, though it concerns my person too, concerns to no lesser extent the totality of those who have been for eighty years and continue to be the advocates of a certain doctrine and point of view that are currently the topic of lively discussions, and since it seems possible that I may be able to be in some way of help in regard to that part of it which depends on familiarity with the scientific truth, I cannot and must not fail to stand ready to be of help in this manner as my conscience as a zealous and Catholic Christian bids me do."

In his eager endeavor to win support for the Copernican thesis, Galileo finally abandoned the reserve he had heretofore imposed upon himself and hesitated no longer to speak up in favor of it in the numerous discussions that he had in Rome. This fact is apparent from a report written by Monsignore Querenghi under date of December 30, 1615: "We have here," Querenghi observed, "a man by name of Galileo Galilei who often, at gatherings of friends of science, speaks amazingly on the opinions of Copernicus which he considers to be true. These gatherings commonly take place at the home of Signor Cesarini and are arranged by Signor Virginio who is a young fellow of extraordinary talents."

On January 20, 1616, the same Querenghi wrote: "This Galileo would delight you if you could hear him speak as he often does, surrounded by fifteen or twenty attackers, all ready to go in for the kill, sometimes in one house and sometimes in another. But he is so well grounded that he can laugh at them all. And even though he may fail to make converts for his new-fangled notions, he does show how worthless most of the arguments are by means

of which his opponents try to fight him. Last Monday, in particular, at the house of Signor Federico Ghisilieri, he was in splendid
form. What I liked especially was his way of not answering his
opponents' arguments directly but of first carrying them farther
to impart to them by means of additional points the highest degree
of probability and of then proceeding to disprove them with the
effect that his opponents looked only the more ridiculous."

Yet while Galileo was still seeking to save the cause of Copernicus, preparations were under way which were to come to a head
in the form of the final decision, prompted perhaps precisely by
Galileo's open advocacy. On February 19, 1616, the Pope requested the theologians of the Holy Office to give an opinion on
two theses. These were:

"The sun is the center of the universe and hence immobile
in terms of local movement."—"The earth is not the center of
the universe and not immobile but moves relative to itself also in
a daily movement."

The verdict was reached in short order. As early as February
24, the Pope was informed with respect to the first of the two
theses that is was absurd and heretical, for it expressly contradicted the wording and interpretation of Holy Scripture, and with
respect to the second thesis the verdict declared that it was in any
event erroneous in faith.

The wording of the two theses, which in fact do not correctly
represent the Copernican doctrine, and also the speed with which
the theologians arrived at their conclusion make it quite clear
that the issue was not at all considered to be a matter of science
requiring an examination of scientific arguments but that all that
was wanted was the explicit formulation of a condemnation that
had all along been taken for granted for ultimately theological
reasons. Under the title of "censure of the assertions of the mathematician Galileo Galilei," the verdict of the Holy Office went into
the records of the General Congregation of the Inquisition.

Pursuant to these findings, Cardinal Bellarmin was charged
with summoning Galileo on February 26, 1616, for the purpose
of informing him that he had to abandon his erroneous stand and
would no longer be allowed to defend it through his teaching or

otherwise. In case he failed to comply with this order he would be thrown into prison.

Galileo submitted to this information, and thus the procedures against him personally were concluded. It was only on March 5, 1616, that the decree of the Congregation of the Index against the writings of Copernicus and his followers was released for publication. The wording of this decree is as follows: "Whereas the Holy Congregation has been apprised that the false Pythagorean doctrine of the movement of the earth and the immobility of the sun, which clearly runs counter to Holy Scripture but which Nikolaus Copernicus teaches in his book, *De Revolutionibus orbium coelestium* . . . , has been gaining ground and is being accepted by many, as may be seen from the printed letter of a certain Carmelite friar bearing the title, *Lettera del R. P. Maestro Paolo Antonio Foscarini Carmelitano, sopra l'opinione die Pittagorici e del Copernico della mobilità della Terra e stabilità del Sole, et il nuovo Pittagorico Sistema del Mondo. In Napoli per Lazzaro Scorriggio 1615*, in which the afore-named Father undertakes to show that said doctrine of the immobility of the sun in the center of the universe and of the mobility of the earth is in accordance with truth and not counter to Holy Scripture, now, therefore, in order to assure that such an opinion may not achieve further insinuation to the detriment of Catholic truth, the Congregation decrees that the aforementioned book by Copernicus, *De Revolutionibus orbium coelestium* . . . , is to be suspended unless and until it is corrected, and that the book of the Carmelite P. Paolo Antonio Foscarini is to be wholly forbidden and condemned, as are all other books which equally teach the same doctrine, in keeping with which the Holy Congregation, through the present decree, forbids and condemns and suspends them in their entirety."

The document condemning the books referred to as well as a number of other books concerned with unrelated subjects carried as a preamble a reminder of the general rules that "no one, regardless of his station or rank, under the penalties provided for at the Council of Trent and in the Prohibitory Index, should undertake to print or have printed said writings or to hold them

in any way in safekeeping or to read them, and, under the same
penalties, those who now have those writings in their possession
or who shall have them in their possession in future should recognize it as incumbent upon them to deliver said books, as soon as
they are apprised of the present decree, into the hands of the
competent authorities or inquisitors."

All this constitutes a sweeping and uncompromising condemnation of the Copernican hypothesis. Yet, however unmistakably
clear this fact may be, no less so is the endeavor to spare the
person of Galileo. There is, first of all, the striking detail that the
decree mentions a document written by a Father Foscarini but
not a single work of Galileo's. When rumors began to be afoot
that Galileo had not simply been reprimanded but had been
obliged to recant, Cardinal Bellarmin was immediately ready to
provide at Galileo's request a statement covering the events as
they had actually happened. The wording of this statement is as
follows: "We, Robert, Cardinal Bellarmin, declare that slanderous rumors have reached our ear claiming, contrary to the truth,
that Galileo has been made to swear off at our hands and was
hence called upon to do penance for the good of his soul. Complying with a request to bear witness as to the true facts, we herewith
declare that the afore-named Galileo has not, either at our hands
or at the hands of anyone else, either in Rome or in any other
place, been made to swear off, as far as our knowledge extends,
any of his opinions or doctrines and that he has not been called
upon to do penance in any shape or form for the good of his soul,
the truth being merely that he has been apprised of a declaration
issued by the Holy Father and published by the Holy Congregation of the Index to the effect that the teachings imputed to
Copernicus may neither be defended nor maintained."

The Pope himself was still willing to grant Galileo an audience that did, in fact, come to pass as we know from a letter
written by Galileo on March 12, 1616, to Minister Vinca: "I explained [to the Pope]," Galileo reported, "why I had come to
Rome, and when I mentioned as part of this explanation how on
taking leave of my prince and master I had renounced any and
every kind of favor he might have been able to grant me, since
I wished to avail myself of none such whenever and wherever

matters of religion or of righteousness of conduct and morals were
involved, His Holiness commented on this decision of mine with
great and repeated praise. I presented to His Holiness proof of
the malice of my detractors emphasizing one and another of their
slanderous imputations. In reply the Pope averred that my probity
and the sincerity of my attitudes were well known to him. Finally,
when I intimated that I was still not completely at ease because
I feared that the same relentless malice would continue to per-
secute me, the Pope reassured me, saying that I had good reason
to live confidently, for the impression which His Holiness and
the entire Congregation had formed of me was such that my
detractors would not find it easy to obtain credence and that, as
long as he lived, I need have no worry. And before I left, the Pope
confirmed repeatedly that he was indeed inclined to use every
occasion to provide, through his actions, evidence of the good
will that he bore me."

It was the Pope's good will, of which Galileo had thus personally been assured, that induced him to stay on in Rome and
to continue there his efforts on behalf of a cause which, in fact,
was already lost. Only the insistent and repeated urgings of the
Grand Duke's court prevailed upon him to terminate his six-
month sojourn in Rome and to return to Florence. There the
situation was evaluated much more realistically, as appears from
a letter which the Secretary of State Piccena addressed to Galileo:
"You have had," Piccena wrote, "a taste of the persecutions of
the monks, and you know what they are like. Our Highnesses
fear that your continued presence in Rome may cause you annoyances, and they would therefore approve heartily, since you
have so far come out on top, if you would desist now from teasing
the dog while it sleeps and return home instead as soon as you
can, for there are rumors abroad of a kind which is not desired,
and the power of the monks is boundless."

For seven years Galileo remained silent. He published nothing. He wrote for the record, vaguely hoping that conditions
would change and that he would then be able to say and uphold
what he believed to have recognized as the truth. Yet even during
these years of solitude he was intent on keeping friendly men of
science apprised of the results of his studies. Some of his detailed

reports, of which numerous copies went from hand to hand throughout Europe, have come down to us. They reflect the dilemma of a searcher after the scientific truth who felt, on the one hand, the urge to disseminate his newly won insights but who, on the other hand, did not wish to be a scandal to the authorities of the Church, for he was both a good Catholic and a man concerned about his personal safety.

When in August 1623 Cardinal Maffeo Barberini succeeded as Urban VIII to the Holy See of Peter, the time seemed to be ripe for a new sally. Cardinal Barberini was known as a friend of science who had not hesitated to speak up in favor of Galileo. So then, in April 1624, Galileo, now sixty years old, once again started for Rome in order to prevail upon the new Pope to effect a revision of the decree of 1616. Galileo was granted six audiences by Urban but did not succeed in inducing the Pope to revoke the decree. The Pope strove to convince Galileo that the decree merely forbad the claim that the Copernican system was more than a hypothesis but not the theoretical discussion of the various Copernican theses. Beyond this the Pope lavished on Galileo assurances of his personal favor, promised him an income for his son, gave him as a gift a painting and two medals, and wrote to the Grand Duke: "It has been a long time since we first embraced in paternal love this great man whose name reflects from the heavens and strides across the earth, for we recognize in him not only the shining light of his learning but also the zeal of his piety. He is rich in the kind of knowledge that easily wins our papal benevolence. Now then, that he has come to Rome to present to us his felicitations on our accession to the papal dignity, we received him in great love and listened to him with delight on repeated occasions as he increased the brilliance of Florentine eloquence in learned disputations. It is unthinkable to us that he should be allowed to return to the city where he has made his home without a rich farewell gift of papal love . . ." And the missive concludes: "All the good that you, noble prince, may bestow upon him will afford us great satisfaction."

It is not hard to understand that Galileo, backed by the evident good will of the Pope and convinced of the Pope's liberality, now set to work to gather together his scientific insights in a book which, to be sure, kept up the formal appearances of a merely theoretical discussion of the Copernican system but which, none-theless, did embody all the proofs and arguments in support of the claim of its undeniable truth. The book consists of *Dialogues on Greatest World Systems*, in which three participants discuss the pros and cons of the Aristotelian and of the Coperni-can cosmologies.

Because Galileo ascribed particular cogency to the phe-nomena of ebb and tide as evidence in support of the Copernican doctrine, he at first called the work, when it was completed in 1629, *Ebb and Tide of the Sea*. This would indeed have been tantamount to a public profession of his pro-Copernican position. Galileo visited Urban again in May 1630. Having been told about the work, Urban objected to the proposed title, and this induced Galileo to give it the less suggestive title under which it is now known.

"It is the will of our lord and master," Father Riccardi wrote to the Inquisitor at Florence on May 21, 1631, "that ebb and tide should not be referred to in the title as the subject of the book but that it be exclusively a mathematical review of the Coperni-can hypothesis of the movement of the earth, undertaken for the purpose of proving that—if the revelation of God and the doc-trine of the Holy Church are left out of consideration—the ob-served events might well be accounted for on the basis of this assumption, with due attention paid to the refutation of all the opposing arguments that might be adduced from experience or from peripatetic philosophy, so that the absolute truth of this view will never appear to have been admitted but only its hypo-thetical possibility, and always without reference to Scripture. It is also to be pointed out that it is the sole purpose of this work to show that all the arguments that can be adduced in favor of this view are well known and that it is not for lack of awareness of what these arguments are that this verdict has been promul-gated in Rome."

The *Dialogues* finally appeared in February 1632, duly pro-vided with the imprimatur of the Roman and Florentine censors. However, it was only a few months later, in August of the same year, that Rome came out with its revocation. The distribution of the book was to cease and all copies within reach were to be impounded.

What had happened?

We must realize that the outcome of the Galileo affair depended on three components: the overall situation of the Catholic Church at the time, the pattern of intellectual and political trends at the Vatican, and—finally—the personal attitude of the Pope. The Church found itself in a precarious situation. In 1629, as the result of a struggle of eleven years' duration, the scales of history appraising the contending forces in the Protestant and Catholic camps had appeared—definitively at last—to give Rome the edge. In the so-called Edict of Restitution (of March 6, 1629), Emperor Ferdinand II had decreed the restoration of all Church property taken by or awarded to the Protestants since the time of the Passau Treaty of 1552. Then, in 1630, King Gustavus Adolphus of Sweden appeared on the European scene, defeated the Imperial Armies in the course of the next two years, and forced his way into German lands all the way to Würzburg, Bamberg, and Mainz. In this situation, Urban did not pursue a policy of alignment with the Emperor but tried, along with Richelieu and the Catholic Prince Electors, to prevent any and every extension of the imperial might and to impose Rome's claim to power not only in religious but also in political terms. The Pope's stance of opposition to the Emperor, in the determination of which Catholic interests were of lesser importance than political considerations of power politics, preoccupied him to such an extent that he tolerated, not to say, approved, Richelieu's deals with Holland and the remaining Protestant countries. Urban resisted Ferdinand's urgent request that he should declare the war a war of religion. Small wonder, then, that the clergy and the population at large were receptive to the suggestion that the Pope was more interested in strengthening his position as a secular ruler than in protecting and increasing the Catholic faith.

At the Vatican itself, Aristotelians were numerically in the majority, and there was little doubt but that they were merely waiting for an opportune moment to bring about Galileo's fall. Their reserve in the face of Urban's initial attitude of benevolence toward Galileo may be accounted for by the fact that the Pope, on the one hand, had built up for himself a buttressing system of personal power by investing relatives of his with important offices in the Roman Curia and that, furthermore, he had made substantial concessions, both in financial terms and in terms of political power and influence, to the Congregations which were dominated by the Jesuits.

Urban VIII was a self-willed prince of the Church, imbued with the conviction that he, in all things, was the first and the wisest. His relationship to literature and science was determined by the wish to stand in these secular matters too as an expert, an initiate, a friend of the great of his age. His major interest was to provide members of his family with positions of power and great monetary yield and, in this way, to secure for himself the supreme might of an absolute sovereign. After his death in 1644, his successor, Pope Innocent X, instituted shortly after his enthronement an investigation against the Barberinis. Their possessions and revenues were confiscated, and finally—on February 20, 1646—the family of Urban VIII was publicly condemned.

It was against this background that the struggle for and against the imprimatur for the *Dialogues* was carried out. The documentation on the events that took place between 1630 and 1632 is too scanty to make it possible for us to determine what influences were at work preventing for so long a favorable decision despite the fact that the Pope favored the release of the work at least in principle and despite the favorable attitudes of both the Roman Censor, the Dominican Riccardi, and the competent Florentine authority. Even if we consider that a whole series of individuals and administrative offices had to examine the manuscript and that at just that time, in 1630, the plague broke out in Italy, greatly interfering with postal communications between cities and raging with unusual violence in Florence when the *Dialogues* were ready to go to press, we still find it difficult to account for this long delay unless we assume that the censors had certain qualms about releasing the work.

Indeed, the *Dialogues* did present a problem. In the preface Galileo explained, in keeping with the Pope's wishes that the arguments in support of the Copernican hypothesis had been gathered together only in order to show the world that the decree

of 1616 was not due to ignorance but had been issued in full
awareness of the supporting proof. "It is for this reason," Galileo
wrote, "that in these *Dialogues* I take the position of the Coperni-
cans. Strictly adhering to the principle of viewing the Copernican doctrine as a mathematical hypothesis, I proceed to show
its superiority, not over the Ptolemaic doctrine as such, but over
the arguments which are adduced in support of it by certain
peripatetic partisans who share with philosophers only the name."
Yet, despite this indubitably skillful introduction, the arguments
favoring the Copernican system predominate to such an extent
and are so strikingly presented as appealing, among the three
speakers, to the two who stand out by their intellectual superiority
that it is impossible to read the work as a whole as anything other
than a passionate endorsement of Copernicus. To make matters
worse, there was a bad formal slip. The *Dialogues*, as stated before, operate with three speakers: the scholar Salviati representing Galileo's position, the alert and well-informed layman
Sagredo, and Simplicio representing the Ptolemaic-Aristotelian
school. Now, this Simplicio was not only endowed by Galileo with
at best modest powers of mind and speech, he was also chosen to
present the statement of God's omnipotence that the Pope had
asked for and, in fact, had formulated himself: "Even though the
Copernican system may seem to be more correct than the system
of Ptolemy, the conclusion that the Copernican system is true
must still be deferred, for such a conclusion is tantamount to
placing God under duress."

Galileo's enemies must have found it easy to refer to this
passage in order to convince the Pope that the figure of this naive
Simplicio was intended to represent him and that it was he who
was being ridiculed in Simplicio's person. It is quite possible that
the proceedings against Galileo would have been reinstituted
even if Galileo had handled this detail more wisely. But it is
probable that in that case the Pope would not have made the
persecution of Galileo his personal concern to the extent that he
did. When the Florentine envoy went to see the Pope in September 1632, that is to say, shortly before the time when the order
forbidding further sales of the *Dialogues* was issued, he ran into
stubborn opposition when he tried, in discussing this matter, to

argue in defense of Galileo. Urban was no longer inclined to spare Galileo but insisted on having proceedings instituted against the 68-year-old gravely ill scientist. On October 1, 1632, Galileo was ordered to appear before the Congregation of the Holy Office in Rome. His petition for a postponement motivated by his poor state of health, the dangers of the plague, and the approach of winter, was rejected.

Galileo's reaction to this unexpected collapse of all the hopes he had placed in Urban's papal regime may be seen from a letter he addressed in quest of help and advice to a cardinal, likewise of the Barberini family, whom he could still regard as a friend. "When I consider," Galileo wrote there among other things, "that the fruit of all my studies and all my efforts now comes down to not more than a summons to appear before the Holy Office, of a kind issued only to those found guilty of grave misconduct, I cannot but incline to curse the time which I devoted to these studies hoping thereby to rise somewhat above the routinely trod paths of science, I cannot but regret that I shared with the world part of my findings and feel the urge to suppress what I still have in my hands, to throw it into the fire in order to satisfy every last wish of my enemies to whom all my thoughts appear to be so very obnoxious."

The closing words of the letter: "If this high and holy tribunal cannot see a sufficient cause for granting me a dispensation (or at least a respite) in either my advanced age or my many physical ailments, in either the deep sorrow which fills me or the hardships of so long a journey under the present most unfavorable conditions, I shall take to the road placing obedience above life."

On December 9, the Inquisitor in Florence was commanded by the Pope to force Galileo to leave for Rome within at most one month. When this delay had passed while Galileo still failed to prepare for the journey but kept claiming that he was ill, the Inquisitor had him examined by three renowned physicians. We have the testimony of these physicians. They found "that Galileo had a pulse intermitting once every three or four beats, that he suffered bouts of vertigo and states of melancholy, and that his ailments included loss of stomach tone, sleeplessness, and saltatory bodily pains." The testimony further avers that Galileo had a hernia and that this was the cause of an involvement of the peritoneal sac.

In Rome the report was lent little or no credence. Urban sent a commissary and a physician who was to report on the state of Galileo's health. They arrived in Florence with the instructions that, if they found that Galileo was able to travel and still refused to obey they were to take him prisoner and bring him to Rome in chains. The papal orders further provided that the commissary and the physician were to travel at the expense of Galileo because Galileo had failed to comply with the order to appear in Rome at a time when his condition provided no semblance of a justification of his not doing so.

Now even the Grand Duke was unable to intercede, and so Galileo started out for Rome on January 26, 1633. Shortly before this time he wrote full of bitterness to a friend: "I heard from a well-informed source that the Jesuits have made it known to those in power that they regard my book as more detestable and as more detrimental to the Holy Church than the writings of Luther and Calvin. And all this despite the fact that in order to obtain the imprimatur I personally went to Rome . . ."

On February 13, Galileo arrived in Rome taking up quarters, at the behest of the Grand Duke, in the palace of the Florentine envoy Niccolini. Although he had been urged time and again to hasten and although he had finally been virtually forced to come, weeks and weeks were now allowed to go by without a sign of any kind of official awareness of his being present. Visits from friends and patrons who promised to intercede on his behalf with the Pope awakened in him the hope that there might still be a possibility of saving his cause. On the other hand, having to wait so long for a response or a summons did wear down his strength. A letter written by the envoy Niccolini on April 8, 1633, described Galileo's condition in the following terms: "Signor Galilei remains convinced in spite of everything that he will be able to defend his assertions with sound reasons. I have urged him to abstain from any attempt of this kind in order to prevent the proceedings from dragging on still longer but to submit to whatever he may be ordered to believe with respect to the movements of the earth. This has cast him into a state of profound sadness and has caused him from one day to the next to lose strength to such an extent that I have the greatest concern for his life."

It was only on April 13, 1633, that the first hearing took place at the headquarters of the Congregation of the Holy Office. In order to understand what occurred between the time of this hearing and Galileo's ultimate condemnation on June 22, 1633, one must know the history of the document forming the principal basis of both the accusation and the verdict, although it is true that certain phases of that history have remained obscure to this day. The statement that, at Galileo's request, Cardinal Bellarmin had provided on the import of the decree of 1616 represented—it will be recalled—an unqualified denial of the "slanderous rumors" then abroad, claiming "that Galileo had been made to swear off" certain of his beliefs and "that he had been called upon to do penance." The statement further insisted, in positive terms, that with respect to Galileo no action had been taken other than that he had "been apprised of a declaration issued by the Holy Father and published by the Holy Congregation of the Index" constituting a decree in accordance with which "the teachings imputed to Copernicus must neither be defended nor maintained."

Now, however, there appeared—in the very first session of April 13, 1633—a reference to an entry in the minutes of February 26, 1616, claiming that Galileo was ordered by word of mouth "that he must abandon once and for all the aforementioned opinion that the sun is the center of the universe and hence immobile while the earth moves and that he must no longer consider true, teach, or defend said opinion either in words or in writing lest the Holy Office take up proceedings against him, which order the same Galileo showed himself satisfied to accept with the promise to comply with it."

While the papal release of February 25, 1616, indicated that such an order would be given "if Galileo should refuse to heed Cardinal Bellarmin's exhortation," the entry in the minutes of February 23, 1616 (as referred to on April 13, 1633), would tend to prove that Galileo was not simply urged in general terms to comport himself in a way consistent with the decree of February 23, 1616, in which Copernicus was condemned but that Galileo

was "ordered and expressly held" to refrain from as much as
discussing the Copernican doctrine and that this was done "in
the presence of the General Commissary of the Congregation of
the Holy Office, Michael Angelo Segnitius de Lauda."

The transcripts of the proceedings show that Galileo denied
time and again that he ever received an order of the kind referred
to. That he was correct in his denial appears to be borne out not
only by Cardinal Bellarmin's statement but also by the fact that
he—Galileo—in the course of the proceedings of 1616, never
thought of acting counter to the papal admonition conveyed to
him by the Cardinal so that the interdiction threatened as a consequence of his noncompliance did not at any time come into
force. The document in question, dated February 26, 1633, was
never presented to Galileo, and he was never asked to acknowl-
edge that it presented the facts as they had actually occurred. The
existence of it became known only in 1867, when the French
scholar Henri de L'Epinois obtained permission to copy and to
publish the material in the archives of the Vatican relative to the
case of Galileo. The controversy as to whether this document is
genuine or a forgery remains undecided even now. It is quite
possible that the document as such was indeed included in the
files as early as 1616 (though it reported an event that never occurred in this precise form) with the idea that the manipulated
interpretation might come in handy as a means to get at Galileo
in case the warning issued against him should prove ineffectual.
On the other hand, it is equally possible that the document—with
or without the Pope's connivance—was produced only in the summer of 1633, when it was found that the material on record did
not suffice to support an indictment accusing Galileo of having
unequivocally violated a papal command. In any event, the order
of February 26, 1616, did not show up till after the proceedings
against Galileo in 1633 were well under way. It bears no signature,
and no seal is attached to it. These latter facts would seem to make
it impossible to assign to the document the character of a valid
record, but this did not prevent it from being utilized as the
principal evidence against Galileo.

After the first hearing in 1633, and especially after the appearance of the ominous document just described, Galileo was

obviously ready to fear the worst, and from the second session
on April 30 on, he saw his only possible salvation in admitting
everything. In this he was quite evidently motivated by the hope
that a full confession would lead to a more or less rhetorical condemnation, that is to say, to that second admonitory phase provided for by Pope Paul V in 1616 as a modality to be invoked in
the event that Galileo did not heed Cardinal Bellarmin's request.
Galileo's readiness to admit that he had done wrong was prompted
in particular by a conversation he had on April 27 with the
Commissary General of the Holy Office, Firenzuola. From this
conversation Galileo had concluded that the authorities were prepared to treat him with forebearance once he admitted that he
had emphasized in his *Dialogues* somewhat too exclusively the
positive aspects of the pro-Copernican arguments. He declared
himself ready to write another dialogue in which he would clearly
and unmistakably disprove the Copernican system.

In the course of the following days, however, Galileo came
to be more and more convinced that a confession on his part
would only be used to justify the harshest measures against him.
A report on the proceedings, which bears no signature but forms
part of the official record and was submitted to the Pope and the
cardinals sometime in the middle of May, proves that this time
Galileo was right. In the report the attitude assumed by Galileo
at the time of the second hearing is interpreted entirely in his
disfavor. Galileo must have been aware of this turn of events.
There was also the fact that, contrary to a promise that he thought
was implied in a statement by Firenzuola, he was retained in the
building which housed the Holy Office and was not allowed to
return to the palace of the Florentine envoy Niccolini. Under
these conditions Galileo considered it wise to present at the time
of the third hearing, on May 10, a writ of defense in which he
expressly referred to the affidavit of Cardinal Bellarmin of May
26, 1616, in which it was stated, to be sure, that the doctrine
ascribed to Copernicus of the movement of the earth and the
fixed position of the sun must not be upheld or defended but
that—to quote Galileo's wording in his writ of defense of May 10,
1633—"aside from this general formula applicable to all, there
is in this testimony no trace of an injunction additionally and spe-

cifically imposed upon me. Since I found myself in possession of this authentic testimonial written for me as an aide-mémoire by the very man who had informed me of the ruling, I gave no further thought to the specific terms used when the order was orally presented to me nor did I strive to keep them in my memory so that the expression 'to teach' (following 'to maintain' and 'to defend') and the qualification 'in whatever way' (*quovis modo*) impress me as entirely new and as things which I never heard before."

It seems that in the course of the following six weeks, that is, up to the time of the next session on June 22, Galileo again felt encouraged and hopeful. This seems to have been due in particular to the fact that after the third session on May 10 he was again permitted to return to the palace of the Florentine envoy. Niccolini, the envoy, succeeded in fact in making it possible for Galileo to take walks in the gardens of the Medici villa, though he had to be taken there in a closed carriage.

As to the character of the negotiations taking place in the course of these decisive weeks from the last hearing to the final reading of the verdict of the Holy Office, we can do no more than venture intelligent surmises. It seems certain that there was a strong group of consultants and of members of the Inquisition, led by the Jesuits and enjoying no doubt the advantage of being listened to by Urban, that was of the opinion that the Church, in the extremely precarious situation in which it found itself at the time, could not afford to be lenient toward a new heresy and that Galileo, being the leader of the Copernican school, had to be "neutralized." It appears, furthermore, that various individuals indirectly in a position to influence the proceedings against Galileo had personal motives to wish his defeat to be clear and complete. These were Aristotelian scholars whom Galileo had so often attacked and ridiculed and who had not proved able to measure up to his scientific and intellectual superiority. It is quite possible that many of these men were simultaneously inspired by a genuine fervor of faith against a scientist who in their opinion was a heretic and whom they were therefore eager to see removed from the scene, although no one doubted at the time or has doubted since Galileo's subjective conviction that he was a pious and faithful son of the Church.

The documentation that has come down to us includes a statement made by the Pope on May 29 to the effect that the *Dialogues* would be forbidden and that Galileo himself would have to recant and do penance. There is, in addition, a verbatim report of discussions taking place on June 16, 1633, indicating that on that day—that is, five days prior to the final session—the verdict had been definitively established in the course of a discussion with the Pope. "His Holiness," the account says, "has commanded that Galileo shall be interrogated relative to the claims pending against him and that he shall be made to recognize that the threat of torture against him is real, whereupon he shall be led to recant in a plenary session of the Congregation of the Holy Office and be sentenced to imprisonment as the Holy Congregation may see fit to decide."

The hearing of June 21, 1633, once again revolved around the question presented by the judges in ever-new formulations as to whether Galileo considered the Copernican doctrine to be true or had ever done so in the past. Galileo's answers leave little doubt as to his determination not to deny his scientific convictions but merely to capitulate before the life-and-limb-threatening power of the Inquisition. According to the minutes of the meeting, one of Galileo's answers was the following: "Prior to the decision of the Holy Congregation of the Index and prior to the time when I was apprised of this order, that is to say, long ago, I was undecided and regarded both views, that of Ptolemy and that of Copernicus, to be worthy of being discussed, for the one as well as the other might prove true in nature, but after the decision, after the time when the wisdom of the superiors gave me certainty, all indecision in me came to an end, and I regarded and still regard as entirely true and hence not subject to doubt the view of Ptolemy that the earth is at rest while the sun moves." Another of Galileo's answers was: "I consider the opinion of Copernicus not to be true and have not considered it to be true ever since I was given orders to abandon it. For the rest, I am here in your hands, and you may do to me whatever it may be your pleasure

to do to me." When the judge asked him once again under the
threat of torture to speak the truth, Galileo answered for the
last time: "I am here to submit. Since the time of the decision I
have not considered this opinion to be true, as I have said."

To the last, then, Galileo insisted on having his recantation
interpreted exclusively as a submission to the authority of the
Church and not as a conversion to the doctrines of the Aristotelians. Despite the all-pervading resignation of his answers, there
is in them an unmistakable vein of determination which suggests
that, even during these most difficult moments marking the final
phase of the proceedings against him, he had decided to give unto
those in power what they asked for and yet not to feel bound in
the matter at issue by the verdict forced upon him or by the recantation forced from him.

On June 22, 1633, the proceedings against Galileo were concluded. In the Church of the Dominican monastery of Santa Maria
Sopra Minerva the Congregation of the Holy Office convened in
solemn session for the purpose of reading in the presence of
Galileo both the indictment and the sentence awarded against
him. The closing words of the latter were: "Yet in order that
your grave and detrimental error and disobedience may not remain unpunished and in order that you may in future proceed
more cautiously and serve at the same time as a warning example
to others, so that they will abstain from similar violations, we
decree that the book of *Dialogues* by Galileo Galilei be forbidden
by a public ruling. We further sentence you to formal imprisonment for a period of time to be determined at our discretion and
demand of you as a wholesome penance that you shall recite once
a week for the term of the next three years the seven penitential
psalms."

Immediately after the reading of the sentence, Galileo was
forced to kneel down and repeat in solemn abjuration the words:
"I abjure, curse, and denounce from an honest heart and in
unfeigned faith all these errors and heresies and withal every
other error and every opinion that is contrary to the Holy Roman
and Roman Apostolic Church. I further swear that I shall in
future neither utter nor maintain either orally or in writing anything that might arouse a similar suspicion of heresy against me.

And should I come to know a heretic or one suspect of heresy, I shall make known his identity to the Congregation of the Holy Office or the Inquisitor or bishop of my diocese."

After this ordeal, Galileo was taken back to the Palace of the Inquisition, but he was kept there only until June 24, when he was allowed, with the Pope's consent, to move to the quarters of the Florentine embassy. The sentence of imprisonment was commuted by Urban to one of qualified confinement. For the time being Galileo was exiled to Sienna where he was placed under the guardianship of the Archbishop Ascanio Piccolomini whom he knew as a friend. A petition of Galileo to be allowed full freedom of movement was turned down by the Congregation of the Index on December 1, 1633, but he was granted permission to return to his villa in Arcetri near Florence. The text of the sentence and of Galileo's abjuration had been published as early as July throughout Italy and the rest of the world, and a warning to all those had been appended who might feel tempted to go on upholding the Copernican doctrine.

In Arcetri Galileo remained under the supervision of the Inquisition up to the time of his death. He was allowed to take walks only in the immediate vicinity of his house, could not receive several persons at the same time, was not allowed to speak for long to anyone, and could never discuss the subject of the movement of the earth. Galileo's illegitimate son Vincenzo (whose mother was the Venetian woman Maria Gamba) was appointed by the Florentine representative of the Inquisition to live with his father and to make sure that all the regulations of the Church were strictly observed. In a letter written sometime later by the Inquisitor to Cardinal Barberini relative to the permission Galileo had been granted to go to see a physician in Florence, we find the following reference to Vincenzo: "He is most appreciative of the clemency accorded his father in the form of the permission that he may be treated by a physician in Florence, and he fears that the slightest violation might result in a cancellation of this permission. Yet it is in his own interest that his father conforms and goes on living for as long as possible, for his father's death will mean to him a loss of one thousand scudi per year, the sum which the Grand Duke continues giving him."

Throughout the last three years of his life, Galileo was also cared for by young Viviani, his later biographer.

In a letter addressed by Galileo to his friend Elio Diodati in Paris he referred to his daughters in the following terms: "Here I now live, keeping calm and quiet, visiting on frequent occasions a nearby convent where two of my daughters used to live as nuns. I loved them dearly, particularly the older one who had outstanding talents of the intellect associated with a rare goodness of the heart. She was deeply attached to me. During the time of my absence, which she regarded as entailing great dangers to me, she abandoned herself to a profound melancholy that undermined her health. Finally she contracted extremely severe dysentery as the result of which she died within six days, only thirty-one years old, leaving me behind in profound sorrow." The day of her death was April 2, 1634.

In the same letter Galileo reported that he had learned from Rome that the Jesuit father Grienberger had stated with reference to him: "If Galileo had known how to maintain himself in the good graces of the Fathers and of the College, he would be living in the world as one crowned with fame, and none of all these adversities would have befallen him. He would have been at liberty to write at will on anything and everything, even on the movement of the earth."—"You see, therefore," Galileo commented on this quotation, "that it was not this or that opinion that drew me into these fights but only the displeasure of the Jesuits."

As for the rest, Galileo did not consider himself vanquished. How little the final outcome of the trial had impaired his vital will and his urge to work and to what extent he regarded his recantation as a false oath forced from him under duress and not, therefore, to be regarded by him as binding, is clearly apparent from the amazing fact that as little as four weeks after the date of the reading of the sentence, that is to say, toward the end of July 1633, he dispatched from Sienna (his first place of exile) the *Dialogues* to the scholar Bernegger in Strasbourg with the request to have a Latin translation of it prepared and published.

There is also the extensive correspondence that he carried on throughout the ensuing years with scholars in other lands and the fact that he used all manner of means available to him in the endeavor to promote the dissemination of his writings outside of Italy, to prove that his capitulation before the life-threatening power of the Inquisition cannot be understood in any sense as indicative of a moral collapse or of cowardice. He observed the external conditions of the qualified confinement imposed upon him, but he never gave thought to the possibility that he might also submit in the matter really at issue.

We know from the utterances of his friends and patrons within and without Italy that have come down to us that Galileo was fully aware of the significance of his scientific discoveries and that he did everything in his power to collect the fruit of his labors in the years he still had left and to have the product printed abroad. It also appears that no one ever undertook seriously to prevent him from pursuing his researches. His son Vincenzo and his disciple Viviani, who shared his exile in Arcetri, as well as the visitors who found their way to him, were content with complying more or less as a matter of form with the regulations of the Inquisition. Scholars throughout Europe accepted Galileo's submission. They knew the power of the Church and had no desire to have the great man fall silent as a hero and martyr at the stake or in prison. They were more interested in having him complete his work. Their resentment, their indignation, and their contempt were leveled at Rome, not at Galileo. Thus the French scholar Fabri de Peiresc noted in a letter addressed to Cardinal Barberini "that a continuation of the exacting procedures against Galileo might well have the effect that future generations come to compare them to the persecution suffered by Socrates." And Hugo Grotius, who regarded the *Dialogues* as the most important book of the century, attempted to have Galileo find safety beyond the confines of the power of the Inquisition and to arrange for his removal to Holland.

It was doubtless this worldwide indignation with the treatment meted out to Galileo by the Church that made the latter consider it wise to dispense with any kind of further proceedings against the aged scholar and to ignore his contacts with the Protestant world, his continued investigations, and the continued dissemination of his earlier and more recent writings. The only thing that was done was that Galileo was prevented from engaging in any kind of public activity inside of Italy and that strict compliance with the rules governing his movements was enforced. Despite the efforts of influential friends of his, Rome was not ready to allow Galileo to move back to his home in Florence although it could not be denied that the medical care which the increasing debility of his state of health would have required was not available to him in the remote rural community of Arcetri. In the course of the year 1637, Galileo became totally blind. The following year he was finally allowed to go to Florence for a few weeks, with the explicit proviso that he was not to discuss the Copernican doctrine with anyone. It was stipulated "on penalty of lifelong imprisonment and excommunication that he should not be free to go out into the City or to speak to anyone, whoever it be, on the cursed doctrine of the double movement of the earth" (letter of Fanano to Cardinal Barberini).

Galileo did not at any time have illusions about the situation he was in. When he received a copy of the letter addressed by Fabri de Peiresc to Cardinal Barberini, he thanked the writer under date of February 22, 1635, noting: "I do not, as I have said, expect any kind of clemency. I do not expect any because I have not committed any kind of crime. I might hope for forgiveness and pardon if I had done wrong, for it is wrongdoing which can provide a prince with the occasion to display clemency and mercy, while it is meet to maintain toward the innocently condemned the whole rigor of the punishment in order to prove that the laws have been complied with in all respects. . . . But believe me, dear sir, and I say so also for the sake of your peace of mind, that this disturbs me less than one might think, for I find at all times strength and consolation from two sources. The one is the knowledge that on examining all my works no one will be able to find even the trace of a shadow of anything deviating from the spirit of love and veneration for the Holy Church. The other is my own conscience which is fully known here on earth only to myself and in heaven to God. He knows that in this matter for the sake of which I suffer . . . no one, not even among the Holy Fathers, would have been able to proceed and to speak with greater piety and greater zeal for the Holy Church or with greater purity of intent."

In the early part of the summer of 1634, the Latin translation of the *Dialogues* readied by Bernegger in Strasbourg appeared in print. Galileo expressed his gratitude in a letter that simultaneously reflects his satisfaction with this triumph. In the preface to this edition there is, to be sure, the explicit statement that it was brought out without the knowledge and against the wishes of the author. Not much later an English translation containing a similar statement appeared. While still in Sienna, his first place of exile, Galileo had begun work on his second major work, the *Discourses and Mathematical Demonstrations of Two New Sciences Concerned with Mechanics and Local Movements* [*Discorsi e dimostrazioni matematichi intorno a due nuove scienze attenanti alla Mecanica e i Movimenti Locali*]. This was the first textbook of physics in which a systematic presentation was attempted of the laws of movement and the behavior of solids. Although this is a purely mathematical and geometric work in which no mention is made anywhere of the Copernican theories, it is precisely this work that must be regarded as a symbol and symptom of the great upheaval, the "Galilean revolution." Prior to this revolution, natural science was wont to describe what could be seen: a "light" leaf falls more slowly than a "heavy" stone. Henceforth, natural science was interested in the laws determining the behavior of falling objects; it discovered the immutable forces underlying all phenomena and came to be in a position to cover by calculations and to reproduce experimentally the diverse conditions leading to diverse phenomenal manifestations. Nature was being secularized; man could see through it, he could dominate it. He no longer depended on what his eyes saw or on the information supplied by the Bible. It was but necessary to ask of nature the right kind of question and to ask correctly and properly, and nature was ready to surrender its secrets.

Toward the end of 1633 Galileo had already sent to his old friend and confidant Fra Fulganzio Micanzio preliminary sketches for the *Discourses* and had asked him to probe the possibility of an Italian edition. When Micanzio approached the Inquisition in Venice in this matter, he was told that the publication of Galileo's works—both old and new—was strictly forbidden in all Catholic countries. After that Galileo undertook various

steps to determine his chances in Austria and Germany. But in
these countries too, no one seemed eager to take such a risk.
Finally, through the mediation of Micanzio in Venice, one of the
first copies of Parts I and II of the finished work was turned over,
once again, to the Dutch book dealer Elzevier when, in the middle
of September of 1636, he personally came to Arcetri from Venice
where he had been attending the book fair. A second copy was
turned over to the Count Noailles, the French envoy to the Vatican, when he, a former disciple of Galileo's was visiting an ac-
quaintance of his in the neighborhood of Arcetri.

The publication of the *Discourses* was delayed until mid-1638.
However, in 1636 an older work of Galileo's, written in 1615, appeared in both the Italian original and a Latin translation prepared once again by Bernegger. This was the detailed analysis
(mentioned before) of the relationship between the Bible and
the Copernican doctrine to which Galileo had given the form of
a letter to the Grand Duchess Christine. This document, addressed as it was to the mother of the later Prince Cosimo, anticipated eighteen years before the time of his trial and of the
sentence against him all the things that moved and concerned
Galileo in regard to the seeming incompatibility of the discoveries of Copernicus with the doctrine of the Church. At that early
time Galileo already was insisting that the truths of Holy Scripture must not be looked for in the Biblical references to facts of
nature and that he was ready at any time to submit to the better
judgment of knowledgeable scholars and theologians if these
proved able to establish the unsoundness of his astronomical observations or their incompatibility with the transcendental veri-
ties of the Bible. Thus the publication of this work represented
to Galileo a belated triumph over his Roman opponents and also
a renewed offensive against them.

In the summer of 1637, Galileo negotiated with a representative of the Dutch States General regarding a nautical exploitation
of his calculations on the orbital revolutions of the moons of
Jupiter which could be used in determining the longitudinal position of a ship at sea. In 1638, the Holy Office brought pressure
to bear on Galileo to induce him to turn down a gift presented
to him by the representative of the States General. He complied,

and Urban expressed to him his personal appreciation of this concession. It may be assumed that Galileo did not find it very hard to be "cooperative" in this matter, for it was in the course of that very same month that the *Discourses* were published by Elzevier in Leiden. It was not long before copies of it were sold in Italy under black-market conditions.

Throughout these last years of his life, Galileo pushed on with might and main to get all his works published and/or translated into Latin. His correspondence on this score was voluminous. As for the rest, "he wished to live out in silence the remainder of his rich and fateful life, enjoying the products of other exceptional minds." These are words quoted from a letter addressed by Galileo on January 7, 1639, to Baliani. To the end Galileo followed with alert interest the work of his disciples, whom he criticized, advised, praised, and encouraged.

On January 7, 1642, he died, having received the blessing of Urban VIII. At his deathbed stood his son Vincenzo, his daughter-in-law Sestilia Boccerini, his disciples Toricelli and Viviani, the local priest, and two representatives of the Inquisition.

It was not until 1822 that the Congregation of the Index decided to tolerate henceforth the publication of works concerned with the Copernican system, and not until 1832, on the occasion of a revised edition of the Prohíbitory Index, were the works of Galileo stricken from the list of forbidden books. On November 4, 1964, Monsignore Elchinger, Coadjutor Bishop of Strasbourg, moved at the Vatican Council that the trial of Galileo be reopened with a view to effecting a solemn rehabilitation of Galileo by the Church.

An Excerpt from Galileo's
Dialogues on the Greatest World Systems

SAGREDO: ... If my memory serves me well, our main concern in yesterday's conversation was that we strove to probe thoroughly the question of which of the two opinions is the more probable and the more firmly grounded—the opinion that

holds the substance of the celestial bodies to be exempt from
generation, destruction, alteration, or sensitivity, to be, in
short, except for its local mobility, subject to no change, representing therefore a fifth element or quintessence entirely
different from our elementary bodies that do undergo regen-
eration, destruction, and alteration, or the opinion that ac-
knowledges no such discrepancy between the parts of the
world and holds instead that the earth enjoys the same qualities as the other bodies constituting the universe or, otherwise stated, that the earth is a freely mobile sphere as are the
moon and Jupiter or Venus and every other planet. We observed in particular that there are many concordances between the earth and the moon—with the moon rather than
with any other planet by reason, presumably, of the more
precise and concrete knowledge we have of it owing to its
greater proximity. Since we finally arrived at the conclusion
that we should regard this second opinion as being of greater
probability, it appears to me that we cannot now do otherwise than proceed with examining the question as to whether
the earth must be regarded as immobile, as it has been believed to be by most so far, or as movable, in keeping with the
belief of some ancient philosophers which is held again by
some men at the present time, and as to the nature of its movement in the event we conclude that it must be regarded as
movable.

SALVIATI: The way we must proceed from here is now quite clear
to me. But before we start out again, I wish to add a few words
to your last remarks in which you stated that we had come
to the result that the opinion that imparts to the earth the
same properties of movement as to the celestial bodies is more
probable than that which opposes it. This is not what I said,
as little as I shall regard any other doctrine of a controversial
nature as demonstrated. My purpose was exclusively to ad-
duce for and against the two opinions the arguments and
counterarguments, the objections and rejoinders that others
have advanced so far and add some new points that have
come to my attention by dint of much thinking, but always

with the understanding that I leave the decision to the judgment of those superior to me.

SAGREDO: You are right, I was carried away by my own interpretation. In the belief that others must judge as I do, I assumed to be universally valid what I should have expressed as a particular view. In this I was wrong, especially since I do not know the attitude of our good friend Simplicio who is here together with us.

SIMPLICIO: I confess I spent all last night turning over in my mind what was said yesterday, and I do find in it indeed much that is beautiful, surprising, and appealing by its boldness. Still, I continue to feel bound by the authority of so many great writers, especially that of. . . . You are shaking your head, Signor Sagredo, you are smiling as though I had uttered an enormity.

SAGREDO: I am smiling, to be sure, but believe me the effort it costs me to prevent myself from bursting out laughing comes close to collapsing, for you have reminded me of a delightful incident at which I was present just a few years ago together with several gentlemen who are friends of mine and whom, if you wish, I can still mention by name.

SALVIATI: It will be well that you tell us what happened so that Signor Simplicio may have no reason to think that it is he who gave you that urge to burst out laughing.

SAGREDO: I shall be glad to. One day I was at the home of a highly reputed physician in Venice where people were used to congregating, some for the sake of their studies but others out of curiosity because they wished to see an autopsy performed by an anatomist whose skill and care were surpassed only by his learning. It happened that the day I was there he was searching for the origin and starting point of the nerves regarding which there is a famous controversy between the Galenists and the peripatetics. The anatomist demonstrated how the great trunk of nerves departing from the brain passes down the back of the neck and following the backbone branches out into all parts of the body, with only a very fine threadlike strand arriving at the heart. Having completed this demonstration the anatomist turned to a gentleman whom he knew to be a peripatetic and whose presence had induced him to carry out his dissection and presentation with an extraordinary degree of care, asking him whether he was now satisfied and ready to admit that the origin of the nerves was in the brain and not in the heart. Whereupon the peripatetic, having pondered the question for a while, replied in these words: "You have showed me these things so clearly and so impressively that, if it were not for the fact that the text of Aristotle opposes it, stating clearly that the nerves arise from the heart, I could not but admit that what you have shown me is true."

SIMPLICIO: I would have you know, gentlemen, that this dispute about the origin of the nerves is by no means as closed and settled a matter as some appear to have persuaded themselves.

SAGREDO: Nor will it ever be, I am sure, as long as it finds such dissenters. But what you have just said cannot in any way lessen the extravagance of the peripatetic's reply in which he did not oppose to a clearly seen fact some other fact or a rational argument derived from Aristotle but simply Aristotle's authority and the dictum *"ipse dixit."*

SIMPLICIO: Aristotle would not have come to be regarded as so great an authority if it had not been for the cogency of his demonstrations and the depth of his reasoning. But we must understand him, in fact, not only understand him but be so versed in his books that we have in our minds a perfect image of them, and this to such an extent that everything he ever said is at all times accessible to our recollection. He did not write for the vulgar crowd, nor did he feel it incumbent upon him to line up his syllogisms in methodical order for the benefit of the beginning student. At times his procedure is disconnected, with the proof of a given proposition being placed in a passage which, on the face of it, treats of an entirely unrelated matter. This is why one must have in one's mind a total picture of his works and be able to connect one passage with another, to find the key to one statement in another that is far removed. There is no doubt but that the man who has acquired this skill will know how to derive from his books the demonstration of all that can be known, for there is nothing that is not in them.

SAGREDO: My dear Simplicio, if that scatteration you describe does not tire you and if you believe that you can find the essence of it by puzzling out fitting combinations for all the little fragments, what you and the other gentlemen in the brotherhood of philosophers are doing by means of the texts of Aristotle, I am prepared to do with lines from Vergil and Ovid, concocting from them potpourris by means of which I can explain all the problems of mankind and the sequence of nature. But what am I saying? Why Vergil or any other poet? I have a booklet that is much shorter than Aristotle and than Ovid, but contained in it is every kind of knowledge. It takes but little study to build from it a perfect image of the world. That booklet is the alphabet. There is no doubt but that the man who knows how to combine and put in proper order this and that vowel with one consonant and another can draw from it a most truthful answer to every kind of question, can use it to obtain instruction in all the arts and sciences in just the manner in which the painter manages to use the diversity of simple colors placed separately on his palate, by combining a little of this and a little of that and yet a little of a third, to make people, plants, buildings, birds, and fishes, to reproduce in fact any visible object although there are on his palate no eyes, no feathers, no fins, no leaves, and no stones. Actually none of the things that the painter wants to imitate or any part of them may ever be in reality among the colors on his palate, for with them he wants to be able to represent any of the things that exist, and if there were among them, let us say, feathers, these could not serve him to depict anything but birds or feather dusters.

SALVIATI: I have heard from several gentlemen who are alive and in good health and able to repeat the story that they were present when a professor from a famous university, having listened to a detailed description of the telescope of which he had never seen a specimen himself, explained that this invention was taken from Aristotle. He had a copy of the book he had in mind brought in, paged through it to a certain passage that explains the reason that one can see by day the stars in the heavens from the bottom of a very deep well. And addressing himself to those present he said: "Here you have the well which stands for the tube; here are the dense vapors from which the invention of the crystals was derived; and here finally is the increase in the power of vision resulting from the passage of the rays through a transparent medium of greater density and darkness.

SAGREDO: This way of comprising all that can be known is quite reminiscent of the way in which a block of marble comprises an extremely beautiful statue or even a thousand such. The problem remains that one must know how to discover them. We might as well say that all this is very much like the prophecies of Joachim of Flora or like the oracles of the heathens which can be understood only after the events they predict have come to pass.

SALVIATI: And do not forget the genethliac predictions which can be seen so clearly, once the events to which they pertain have come to pass, in the subject's nativity or, shall we say, in the heavenly constellations.

SAGREDO: It is in this same fashion that the alchemists, guided by their black bile, find that all the most inspired minds of the world have in truth never written of anything other than of the art of making gold. Since they did not wish to divulge their secrets to the vulgar crowd, they figured out the one this and the other that way of concealing them in diverse disguises. It is sheer delight to hear their comments on the ancient poets and on how they have been able to uncover the most enlightening mysteries that are concealed in what to others are poetic fables: what is meant by the loves of Luna, by her descent on earth for the sake of Endymion, her wrath against Actaeon; when and under what conditions Jupiter turned himself into a shower of gold or again into burning flames; and what great secrets of the art are contained in Mercury's messengerdom, in Pluto's rapes, and in the golden boughs.

SIMPLICIO: I grant that there may be—to a certain extent I know as a fact that there is—no shortage in this world of over-wrought minds, but the antics of these must not be allowed to redound to the prejudice of Aristotle of whom, I think, you speak at times with not enough respect. The antiquity of his name and the great repute in which he stands in the minds of so many and of such excellent men should suffice to command respect for him on the part of all the learned.

SALVIATI: That, Signor Simplicio, is hardly the way this thing is running. There are not a few followers of Aristotle who, in their pettiness, are quite willing to denigrate him, or rather, who would be willing to do so if we were willing to applaud them and the vacuities of their thought. But tell me now, are you really simple-minded enough to fail to see that if Aristotle had been present and had heard that good professor trying to make him the inventor of the telescope, he would have felt much greater resentment against the professor than against those others who were ridiculing the professor and his way of interpreting things? Can you seriously doubt that Aristotle, if he were here to see the new discoveries in the heavens, would gladly realign his thinking, revise his books, and endorse these doctrines that have the support of the perception of our senses and that he would forthwith part company with all those sparrow-brained characters who endeavor in their pettiness to declare inviolable every word he ever uttered without understanding that if Aristotle had been the way they picture him he would have been a dullard, a squarehead, a barbarian, a would-be tyrant regarding all his fellows as stupid cattle and insisting that his own dicta take precedence above perceived evidence, above experience, even above nature? It is Aristotle's followers that have invested him with supreme authority. It was not he who usurped it, who arrogated it to himself. And because it is easier to hide behind the shield of another than to come out into the open and take a stand of one's own, they are afraid and do not take a single step away from him. Rather than admit the need for a change in the Aristotelian firmament, they brazenly deny the changes which they see in the firmament of nature.

SAGREDO: Such men remind me of the sculptor who had fash-
ioned from a great block of marble the likeness of, I know
not which, a Hercules or a thundering Jupiter, imparting to
it with his marvelous art so much life and such impressive
grandeur that all who saw it were filled with fright. In the
end the sculptor himself came to be afraid of it though every
lifelike trait and every movement in that likeness was the
work of his own hands. But the fear in him was such that he
would no longer have had the courage to approach his work
with a chisel and a mallet in his hands.

SALVIATI: I have often wondered how it is possible that these
defenders of every last letter in every utterance of Aristotle
do not realize to what extent they harm his reputation and
his standing and how, while striving to increase his authority,
they detract from it, for when I observe how obstinately they
persist in maintaining the validity of Aristotelian proposi-
tions the erroneousness of which they must be able to see
with half an eye and how they try to convince me that theirs
is the demeanor befitting a true philosopher and that Aristotle himself would have proceeded in no other way, I sense a
weakening in me of the notion that Aristotle argues correctly
in matters less familiar to me. Indeed, if ever I found such
men to be willing to give in and change their stand in the
face of a manifest truth, I would find it easier to believe that
in matters where they persist they may be in possession of
reliable information of whose existence I am not aware or
which I do not understand.

SAGREDO: Also, if they fear that their own reputation and that
of Aristotle is at stake when they are asked to admit that
they as well as he were unaware of a discovery made by someone else, why should it be so difficult to trace that discovery
in Aristotle's texts by means of the device, explained by
Signor Simplicio, of fitting together pieces from several of
them? After all, if everything that can be known is in them,
it follows that this new discovery is bound to be contained
in them, too.

SALVIATI: Signor Sagredo, you should not, I think, make fun
of this ingenious procedure that you appear to be propound-

ing as a jest. Not so long ago a philosopher of great renown composed a book on the soul in which, in a discussion of Aristotle's views on whether it, that is, the soul, is or is not immortal, he quoted numerous passages—none of those quoted by Alexander of Aphrodisias, for, he said, in them Aristotle was not concerned with this matter at all nor with anything of decisive significance pertaining thereto, but others that he had himself discovered in hidden places and which reflected a rather pernicious attitude. When this philosopher was advised that he might have difficulties getting permission to have his work published, he wrote back to the friend who had made this point that he should not let it deter him from pursuing the matter as vigorously as possible, for—if that was the only obstacle—he (the philosopher) would have no difficulty whatsoever changing Aristotle's lesson and support by a different approach and with other quotations the opposite opinion which would still be representative of Aristotle's thinking.

SAGREDO: Bravo, that is the kind of teacher one should have! He is nobody's fool, not even Aristotle's. He does the leading, holding Aristotle by his nose and having him speak at his bidding. There we see how important it is to know when and how. It is not wise to tackle Hercules when he is enraged and at the mercy of the furies. One should approach him while he is telling merry tales among the Maeonian maidens. Oh, the unheard-of wretchedness of servile minds! Going into slavery of their own free will, accepting as inviolable the decrees of others, feeling obliged to appear convinced and persuaded by arguments so cogent and so clearly conclusive that those adducing them do not know for certain to what they are relevant and whether they can rightly be used as evidence for this or that conclusion! But the height of the insanity is that those men cannot agree among themselves as to whether the author himself argued for or against it. What is it they are doing if it is not setting up a wooden statue as their oracle? To run to it with questions, to fear it, to revere it, to adore it?

SIMPLICIO: But if we let go of Aristotle, whom have we left to guide us in our philosophical endeavors? Name one, I ask you, just one among the writers we know.

SALVIATI: There is need for a guide in unknown lands or in a rugged wilderness. Through open fields on trodden paths only the blind want to hold onto a leader's hand. But for such it is best that they stay at home. The man who has eyes in his head and is equipped with a seeing mind should not feel in need of another guide. Not that I mean to say that we should not listen to Aristotle. On the contrary, it is praise-worthy to look up what he has to say and to study him with great care. What I object to is merely a procedure that makes us fall prey to him because it demands of us that we blindly subscribe to every word he uttered accepting it as an inviola-ble decree to the exclusion of a search of our own for any other kind of reason. That is an abuse in which inheres the further risk that it weakens a man's endeavor to understand fully the cogency of Aristotle's demonstrations. What can there be more shameful than to see in a public debate con-cerned with demonstrable points of argument how a quota-tion gets dragged in—possibly one that was written with reference to an entirely different subject—and how it is by means of that quotation that the opponent is made to shut his mouth? If you still want to go on studying in this manner, the least you can do is that you relinquish your claim to the title of scholar and thinker. Call yourselves instead historians or doctors in mnemonics. It is not right that a man who never thinks should still lay claim to the honored title of thinker and philosopher. But let us get back to solid ground and not sail on through this boundless sea on a voyage we could not possibly complete before the day is up. So then, Signor Simplicio, let us have your arguments and demonstrations or those of Aristotle, but spare us your references to texts and bare authority, for we are concerned in our discussions with the world of the senses and not with a world of paper.

Bibliographical References

I. Brecht's *Life of Galileo*

Bertolt Brecht: *Leben des Galilei* [Life of Galileo]. Original version written in Denmark in 1938/39, unpublished.

Bertolt Brecht: *Leben des Galilei* [Life of Galileo]. Separate editions of the plays, Berlin (Suhrkamp), 1957 (repeatedly reprinted).

Bertolt Brecht: *Schriften zum Theater* [Writings on the Theater]. Seven volumes, Frankfurt on the Main, 1963-64; also *Schriften zum Theater—Über eine nichtaristotelische Dramatik* [Writings on the Theater—On a Non-Aristotelian Dramaturgy]. Selected essays, Frankfurt on the Main, 1957.

Arnolt Bronnen: *Tage mit Bertolt Brecht* [Days I Spent with Bertolt Brecht]. Munich, 1960.

Martin Esslin: *Brecht—Das Paradox des politischen Dichters* [Brecht—The Paradox of the Political Writer]. Frankfurt on the Main, 1962.

Kurt Fassmann: *Brecht—Eine Bildbiographie* [Brecht—A Biography in Pictures]. Munich, 1958.

Max Högel: *Bertolt Brecht—Ein Porträt* [Bertolt Brecht—A Portrait]. Augsburg, 1962.

Helge Hultberg: *Die ästhetischen Anschauungen Bertolt Brechts* [Bertolt Brecht's Aesthetics]. Copenhagen, 1962.

Marianne Kesting: *Bertolt Brecht in Selbstzeugnissen und Bilddokumenten* [On Bertolt Brecht, by Himself, with Pictorial Documents]. Hamburg, 1959.

Norbert Kohlhase: *Dichtung und politische Moral—Eine Gegenüberstellung von Brecht und Camus* [Creative Writing and Morality in Politics—A Confrontation of Brecht and Camus]. Munich, 1965.

Werner Mittenzwei: *Bertolt Brecht—Von der "Maßnahme" zu "Leben des Galilei"* [Bertolt Brecht—From "The Measures Taken" to "The Life of Galileo"]. Berlin, 1962.

Käthe Rülicke: "Leben des Galilei—Bemerkungen zur Schlußszene" [Life of Galileo—Remarks on the Closing Scene], *Sinn und Form*, Second Special Bertolt-Brecht Issue, Berlin, 1957; also in *Materialien zu Brechts "Leben des Galilei"* [Documentation on Brecht's "Life of Galileo"]. Frankfurt on the Main, 1963.

Ernst Schumacher: *Drama und Geschichte—Bertolt Brechts "Leben des*

Galilei" und andere Stücke [Drama and History—Bertolt Brecht's "Life of Galileo" and Other Plays]. Berlin, 1965.

Fritz Sternberg: *Der Dichter und die Ratio—Erinnerungen an Bertolt Brecht* [Of Reason and Writing—Memories of Bertolt Brecht]. Göttingen, 1965.

Extensive bibliographies of works by and about Brecht will be found in the second special Brecht issue of the periodical *Sinn und Form* as well as in the books by Martin Esslin and Werner Mittenzwei. The latter contains a bibliography of the newspaper and periodical articles on Brecht's *Life of Galileo* up to 1957.

II. The Life of the Historical Galileo

Friedrich Dessauer: *Der Fall Galilei und wir* [The Case of Galileo in a Modern Perspective]. Frankfurt on the Main, 1957 (Fourth Edition).

Karl von Gebler: *Galileo Galilei und die Römische Curie* [Galileo Galilei and the Roman Curia]. Two volumes, Stuttgart, 1876-77.

Leonardo Olschki: *Galilei und seine Zeit* [Galileo and His Age]. Halle, 1927.

Le Opere di Galileo Galilei [The Works of Galileo Galilei]. National Edition, 20 volumes, Florence, 1890-1909.

Ernst Schumacher: *Der Fall Galilei—Das Drama der Wissenschaft* [The Case of Galileo—The Drama of Science]. Darmstadt, 1964.

Emil Wohlwill: *Galilei und sein Kampf für die kopernikanische Lehre* [Galileo and His Fight for the Copernican Doctrine]. Volume I, Hamburg and Leipzig, 1909; volume II, Leipzig, 1926.

All the quotations relative to the life of Galileo have been taken from the two volumes of the work of Emil Wohlwill which was based on the national edition of Galileo's writings.

[TRANSLATOR'S NOTE: The excerpt from Galileo's *Dialogues on the Greatest World Systems* has been newly translated from the original Italian *I Dialoghi sui massimi sistemi*. The Galileo quotations in the text have been translated from the version known to Brecht as found in the two volumes of Emil Wohlwill's German study.]

Notes

1. The concept of "self-alienation" [*Selbstentfremdung*] in Marx is often related to Brecht's *Verfremdungseffekt* [alienation or "exotification" effect] which will repeatedly come up for discussion in these pages. Its incompatibility with Marxist fundamentalism may here at least be alluded to.
2. "Jeder nach seinen Fähigkeiten, jedem nach seinen Bedürfnissen." —Karl Marx, "Kritik des Gothaer Programms" [Criticism of the Gotha Program], in Karl Marx and Friedrich Engels, *Ausgewählte Werke* [Selected Works], Dietz (Berlin), 1953, vol. II, p. 17.
3. Herbert Lüthy, "Vom armen Bert Brecht" [Our Poor Bertolt Brecht], in *Der Monat*, May 1952, p. 134.
4. Sigmund Freud, "Dostojewski und die Vatertötung" [Dostoevski and Patricide], in *Gesammelte Werke* [Collected Works], vol. XIV, p. 400.
5. See "Bibliographical References."
6. *Die Erde bewegt sich.*
7. Hultberg, *op. cit.* (see "Bibliographical References"), p. 205.
8. Mittenzwei, *op. cit.* (see "Bibliographical References"), pp, 330f.
9. *Ibid.*, pp. 255ff.
10. *Ibid.*, p. 255.
11. Schumacher, *op. cit.* (see "Bibliographical References"), pp. 135ff.
12. "Aufbau einer Rolle/Laughtons Galilei," in *Materialien* . . . , p. 60.
13. *Ibid.*, pp. 68f.
14. *Ibid.*, p. 10.
15. *Ibid.*, p. 75.
16. *Sinn und Form*, p. 281.
17. *Materialien* . . . , pp. 61f.
18. *Ibid.*, p. 94.
19. *Ibid.*, p. 118.
20. *Ibid.*, p. 119.
21. *Ibid.*, p. 121.
22. Wolfdietrich Rasch, "Bertolt Brechts marxistischer Lehrer" [Bertolt Brecht's Marxist Teacher], in *Merkur*, October 1963, pp. 988ff.
23. *Hearings Before the Committee on Un-American Activities*, vol. IX, Washington, D.C., pp. 1292-1324.
24. "I never was and am not now a member of any communist party. . . . It is quite possible that something like that was once suggested to me, but I quickly found out that that was not for me."

25. "He is doing very well. He is doing much better than many of the other witnesses you have produced for us. . . . Thank you, Mr. Brecht, you are a good example for the witnesses of Mr. Kenny and Mr. Crum."

26. Schumacher, *op. cit.*, p. 39.

27. Schumacher, "Form und Einfühlung," in *Materialien* . . ., p. 155.

28. *Ibid.*, p. 12.

29. Schumacher, *op. cit.*, p. 57: "It was in keeping with historical realities when [Brecht] showed Galileo as a determined fighter for the restitution of truth and its further dissemination. . . . [The first version] characterized the demeanor of the historical Galileo correctly as that of a man who utilized all legal and illegal possibilities of making up for the damaging effects of his recantation and of going on in his endeavor to convince others of the truth of his convictions."

30. *Materialien* . . ., p. 117.

31. *Sinn und Form*, p. 269.

32. Schumacher, *op. cit.*, p. 168.

33. Schumacher was able to provide proof and documentation for several of his exegetic points imputing to Brecht the conscious objective of presenting definite political theses in his revision of the *Galileo*. This does not hold true for all the points worked out by Schumacher but certainly for a sufficient number to suggest that the play really needs a detailed theoretical blow-by-blow guide to enable the reader to understand it "correctly."

34. *Am Tor des Himmels* [At the Gates of Heaven], Insel (Wiesbaden), 1954, pp. 55ff.

35. Schumacher, *op. cit.*, p. 62: "Brecht does not mention and does not embody in his work the fact that Galileo's subjective endeavor did not comprise the objective of disrupting or destroying faith but only that of securing the recognition of knowledge within the framework of faith, with the implied demand for a reconciliation of the two."

36. Separate editions of the plays, No. 5, p. 170.

37. "Vergnügungstheater oder Lehrtheater," in *Schriften zum Theater* (selected essays), p. 63.

38. "Kleines Organon für das Theater," in *Schriften zum Theater* (selected essays), pp. 139, 140, 151, 158, 165.

39. Edwin Piscator, *Das politische Theater* [The Political Theater], Hamburg, 1963, pp. 132f.

40. "Die Wahrheit ist konkret."

41. *Materialien* . . ., p. 167.

42. *Schriften zum Theater*, vol. I, p. 181.

43. Esslin, *op. cit.* (see "Bibliographical References"), p. 178.

44. *Materialien . . .,* p. 105.
45. *Ibid.,* pp. 110f.
46. *Schriften zum Theater* (selected essays), p. 26.
47. *Ibid.,* pp. 285f.
48. *Schriften zum Theater,* vol. III, p. 28.
49. See Kenneth Tynan, *Argumente und Argumente* [Arguments and Arguments]. Berlin, 1964, p. 25.
50. Referring to the functional reorientation effected in the American version of the *Galileo,* Schumacher, *op. cit.,* p. 172, wrote: "In order to adapt the 'moral' of the play to the new societal situation Brecht did not hesitate to 'tendentialize' the attitudes of the historical Galileo. To be sure, Brecht characteristically looked for a scientific justification of his procedure, in keeping with his profession as formulated in the essay, 'The Theater as Entertainment versus the Theater as a Teaching Institution,' that he 'could not keep going as an artist without help from the sciences.' It is for this reason that he was not content with the complete transposition of historical knowledge into his works. . . . He tried, in addition, to effect a demonstration of the validity of his new evaluation in scientifically theoretical terms, though naturally with reference to the use he had made of it in his play."
51. Erik Erikson, Young Man Luther: A Study in Psychoanalysis and History. New York, 1958, Chapter 5.
52. Bronnen, *op. cit.* (see "Bibliographical References"), p. 30.
53. Sternberg, *op. cit.* (see "Bibliographical References"), p. 8.
54. Alexander Mitscherlich, *Auf dem Wege zur vaterlosen Gesellschaft* [Toward a Fatherless Society]. Munich, 1963, p. 117.
55. Ludwig Marcuse, *Mein zwanzigstes Jahrhundert.* Munich, 1960, p. 131.
56. A classical example of the grotesque naiveté of socialist motivation research is the interpretation applied by Schumacher (*op. cit.,* pp. 350f.), to Brecht's conception of and attitude toward the "heroic." Since communist anthropology considers the individual a sheaf of blank pages onto which social conditions and political ideas can be projected, the motivation of Brecht's antiheroism is made out to have been what in fact was its rationalization after the fact: "The recognition and propagation of a new hero, the proletarian fighter and the people fighting for socialism and peace as a collective hero; the 'real utopia' of an 'era of no heroism' made possible through the creation of a state of society in which heroic comportment as a distinctive attitude is no longer needed."
57. In the notes to his study of *Galileo,* Schumacher mentioned the fact

that in 1937 Brecht followed the Moscow trials with concentrated interest. On the basis of relevant documents in the Brecht Archive, Schumacher concluded "that Brecht became increasingly aware of the existence of a discrepancy between the necessity of defending the proletarian revolution and the necessity of an arbitrary manipulation of law and justice postulated by that revolution but that he never doubted for one moment that the Soviet Union and the Communist Party in the Soviet Union represented the mainstay in the struggle against fascism and would in the end decide the issue" (*op. cit.*, p. 409). According to Schumacher there is reason to assume that in the conception of Galileo's self-accusation and self-accounting in the thirteenth (later fourteenth) scene, Brecht took his cue from reading the closing words of Bukharin who pronounced himself guilty in the third Moscow trial of 1938 (*op. cit.*, pp. 109f).

58. *Materialien* . . ., p. 10.

59. *Ibid.*, pp. 13f.

60. *Ibid.*, p. 47.

61. Cf. Schumacher, *op. cit.*, p. 349: "Work as pleasure, intellectual effort as a sensuous pleasure, sensuous pleasure as a motivation of intellectual effort, these are experiences and modes of behavior which Galileo and Brecht had in common. Shared by Galileo and Brecht were the great 'appetites,' the control of which Brecht in his younger years had in vain been hoping for, the unquenchable thirst for 'world.' . . ."

62. Quoted by Galileo in a letter addressed by him in 1634 to his friend Elio Diodati in Paris.

DATE DUE

MAR 24 1972		
FEB W 1973		
APR 16 '73		
NOV 23 73		
MAY 3 1974		
OCT 25 1975		
OCT 28 1988		
GAYLORD		PRINTED IN U.S.A.